Drone Nation

Drone Nation

The Political Economy of America's New Way of War

Geoff Martin
Erin Steuter

LEXINGTON BOOKS
Lanham • Boulder • New York • London

Published by Lexington Books
An imprint of The Rowman & Littlefield Publishing Group, Inc.
4501 Forbes Boulevard, Suite 200, Lanham, Maryland 20706
www.rowman.com

Unit A, Whitacre Mews, 26-34 Stannary Street, London SE11 4AB

British Library Cataloguing in Publication Information Available

Library of Congress Control Number: 2016956011
ISBN 978-1-4985-4957-8 (cloth : alk. paper)
ISBN 978-1-4985-4959-2 (pbk. : alk. paper)
ISBN 978-1-4985-4958-5 (ebook)

♾™ The paper used in this publication meets the minimum requirements of American National Standard for Information Sciences Permanence of Paper for Printed Library Materials, ANSI/NISO Z39.48-1992.

Printed in the United States of America

Contents

Acknowledgments

A book is a major, multiyear project during which authors accumulate debts of gratitude. For the cover art, we would like to thank artist Simon Robson, also known as Knife Party, for the powerful image entitled *Click Boom*. We are very grateful to Valerie Mansour for collaborating with us in editing this book and preparing it for the publisher's consideration, making the text more accessible, clear, and concise.

Geoff Martin is grateful to Mount Allison University's Senate Committee on Research and Creative Activity, which in 2011–2012 awarded him a research stipend that provided him with some salary support to get a start on this project. These awards for academics in part-time "teaching only" positions are a rarity and it should be a priority across North America to make them more common. He also acknowledges his full-time employer, the Mount Allison Faculty Association, for providing him with a number of research days each year, without which he would not have been able to do his share of this project. Successive presidents and executives of the union have been unstinting in their support.

Throughout this project Geoff Martin has thought often about his ancestors and how they were touched by warfare over the last three hundred years. For his family this starts with the British-French wars of the eighteenth century, culminating in the English decision to expel the Acadian civilians from Atlantic Canada in 1755. Then a New Rochelle, New York, family was divided by the decision of one member, Major John Germain, to fight with the Westchester County militia during the US War of Independence, while the rest of the family migrated as Loyalists in 1783 to what became the Canadian province of New Brunswick. According to a surviving press clipping, another ancestor was present at the "Relief of Lucknow," India, in 1858.

The twentieth century was the era of total war though periods of war were punctuated by even longer periods of nonwar. Many of his ancestors participated in the Great War (1914–1918) and World War II (1939–1945) as members of the Royal Canadian Army. One great uncle, Horace Morell, did not return. These disruptions also had a major impact on the home front, especially for the women and children. As we wrote about the changing nature of air war and of the role of the pilot, Martin thought about his late uncle Capt. George W. Morell, who served in the Royal Canadian Air Force for twenty years starting in the late 1940s. Uncle George never knew combat but he did know about the life-and-death responsibilities of a fighter pilot. All of these people and many since often learned the hard way the truth about war and it is foolhardy for us to forget those truths.

Past wars and periods of relative peace have defined the lives of many of us in surprising ways. But now we appear to be entering a period of permanent war, aided by assassination mainly via ever-proliferating drone aircraft, and we are being led by people very different from past leaders. Whatever the faults of those who were the political leaders of the past, more often than not they did know war firsthand and by 1945 they finally decided that every available step needed to be taken to abolish the war system. We dedicate this work to those who seek to remind contemporary leaders, most of whom have never served, of the uncontrollability and dangers of war.

Introduction

New Way of War

There is an accepted wisdom that democratic, developed countries in the Western world conduct themselves at a higher moral level than others. But the US government, over the last fifteen years, has done things to others, such as kidnapping, torture, and assassination, that only the "bad guys" used to do. Their newest and most alarming tactic is drone warfare—the application of technologically advanced aerial vehicles with no pilot in the cockpit, purportedly capable of precise strikes on the enemy. As a key tool in counter-terrorism strategy, the use of drones is increasing rapidly, along with a corresponding increase in the number of civilian deaths. The title of this book, *Drone Nation*, is no exaggeration.

Normalizing assassination and drone warfare has created a profound historical transformation in the way war is fought that has been evident on this scale only every fifty to seventy-five years. Its significance is equal to transformative events going back a century or further. To put it in the language of French historian Fernand Braudel, the rise of drone warfare means change in the much longer period, the *longue durée*. This technology has a momentum to become the dominant form of military force over the coming decades. It will transform many aspects of life, including a decline in personal privacy and security. In a 2016 article,[1] Josh Smith reports that the United States Air Force (USAF) now clocks as many flying hours with drones as it does with F-16 fighters, one of its past workhorses. When current and retired Air Force personnel speak freely, they sometimes have alarming things to say, far different from the US government's official story on drones. As Smith writes:

Even some proponents, like retired Lieutenant Colonel T. Mark McCurley, a former Air Force drone pilot, say over-reliance on remote killing and electronic intelligence has hurt efforts on the ground. "Too often, remotely piloted aircraft are being used as a tool to wantonly kill individuals, rather than as one of many tools to capture and shut down whole terrorist networks," he said.

While wars have multiple internal and external players, each with a separate agenda, an end to the violence is often created through a combination of a committed citizenry, international pressure, and negotiations. The use of drone warfare, however, may create a much different result. It could actually herald an era of permanent war. Imagine a war that doesn't end, a war that generates continual, extraordinary changes in military and domestic life globally—and one that could require rewriting international law. Whereas twentieth-century international law focused on the long-term relationships between and among nations and states, drone warfare and its new associated policies focus only on the short term—until the next election. There is little regard as to how these intimidating actions will affect the future—for Americans and for citizens of other countries.

Drone Nation provides the opportunity to give these new developments the serious scrutiny they need, before they become regarded as normal Western government policy. The authors have discovered that it is important to focus both on the short-term impact of drone warfare, and to situate it in a much longer historical perspective.

There were warnings as far back as 1976, with the *Senate Select Committee to Study Governmental Operations with Respect to Intelligence Activities,* known as the "Church Committee." It was established following revelations of intrusions into the privacy of American citizens by the CIA, and, perhaps more importantly, the CIA's orchestration of the 1974 overthrow of the democratically elected government of Salvador Allende in Chile. Senator Frank Church (D-Idaho) wrote prophetically in his introduction, speaking for the committee majority: "We regard the assassination plots as aberrations. The United States must not adopt the tactics of the enemy. Means are as important as ends. Crisis makes it tempting to ignore the wise restraints that make men free; but each time we do so, each time the means we use are wrong, our inner strength, the strength which makes us free, is lessened."[2]

The terms *assassination* and *targeted killing* are used carefully in this book. As readers will see, despite the official line, drone killing is most often not very targeted. The term is more likely a euphemism to sanitize what is happening, and to grant key claims of the US administrations of both George W. Bush and Barack Obama that the killing is precise and a sign of military competence.

WE ARE NOT DRONES?

In a discussion about drone warfare, the first issue is what to call these aerial weapons—*unmanned aerial vehicles* (UAV), *unmanned aerial systems* (UAS), *remotely piloted aircrafts* (RPA), or drones. There are strong supporters and detractors for each term. Kevin McCaney points out that the US military (particularly the army and navy) calls them UAV because they are expected to become more autonomous with a declining level of human control.[3] Martin Dempsey, former chair of the Joint Chiefs of Staff, and the most senior US uniformed military leader, argued in May 2014 that the term UAV should be banned because the weapons are not even semiautonomous as it takes eighty personnel to keep each in the air.

Brian Fung reported in the *Washington Post* that drone manufacturers are trying to rebrand them as UAS because the word *drone* has a reputation for showering death from the sky—not helpful in selling Americans on their domestic civilian use.[4]

Advocates of RPA include the USAF and many of its members. For them, despite the distance between pilot and aircraft, these aircraft are piloted to the same degree as those with a flier in the cockpit—there is a remote pilot, sensor operator, and other participants in the loop. As an instructor pilot in the 29th Attack Squadron at Holloman Air Force Base, New Mexico, put it, "Drones get shot at for target practice. We are not drones."[5] However, these machines are mindless and their ability to function is connected to the systems of communication between the aircraft and the pilot. The necessary intimidation is better captured by the value-laden drone than by sanitized terms like UAV, UAS, or RPA. As McCaney and other authors say, the term *drones* will likely always be with us.

CUBE-FARM WARRIORS

The creation of what will truly be a Drone Nation will require a paradigm shift, not only in equipment, but also in how the United States fights in the air, who does the fighting, and how those who fight relate to their aircraft, ground crew, and commanders. Historically, the USAF has been dominated by its pilot corps. The pilots have been at the top of the pinnacle, and senior commanders are primarily drawn from their ranks. Military pilots of fighters, bombers, or transports are highly trained and work in physically demanding jobs. So what happens as the United States makes the transition, and the balance shifts from pilots in cockpits to pilots in overstuffed leather chairs? (The image of a cluster of office cubicles, a cube farm, comes to mind.) And what happens when the pilot has changed from a relatively autonomous decision maker to a cog in the wheel of the new way of war?

At one level, this new attitude to military piloting resembles the shift from custom, craft-based production to industrialization's standardized factory production. In the twentieth-century model, the fighter pilot is like a craftsperson who delivers the entire service, responsible for takeoffs, landings, aerial maneuvers, reconnaissance, and identification. The pilot bunks near his or her plane; in fact it is *his* or *her* plane, as each plane in the squadron had been assigned to a pilot/copilot-navigator duo, with their names inscribed on the fuselage. The pilot is an officer, typically a captain or above but without a body of enlisted people to command. He or she does have power to make awesome decisions of life and death and to apply the laws of war and the rules of engagement. This traditional idea of the pilot is displaced as a quaint, inefficient relic of the past, superseded by new technology as were the unionized pressmen in the newspaper business in the 1970s.[6] Grégoire Chamayou describes the pilot corps as a "military caste on the wane."[7]

Assembly-line mass production of the late-nineteenth and twentieth centuries revolutionized how military equipment was made. State combatants on all sides produced vast quantities of war materiel in the twentieth century. Frederick Winslow Taylor pioneered scientific management—coined "Taylorism"—which was at the root of this revolution. Production could be greatly increased, and labor deskilled, by dividing the process into many small and easy tasks repeated by a large number of unskilled workers. Henry Ford, from the Ford Motor Company, added the concept of the moving assembly line, which again increased productivity. Instead of one craftsperson or a small group doing all tasks necessary to manufacture a product, many lessskilled workers would build the same product through an engineered production process, coined "Fordism." Remarkably, while these ideas revolutionized military production, they have had little impact on the conduct of aviators. Until now.

RISE AND FALL IN US FOREIGN POLICY

One of the features of European-based Western civilization over the last number of centuries is the common, optimistic idea that society continually improves. This spirit of progress, as it is sometimes called, contends that human civilization is on an upward trajectory, that by many measures we are getting better off all the time. The market economy is said to encourage economic growth, human freedom continues to advance, and old gender and racial prejudices are undermined. Advocates of this global view would point to the seeming spread of democracy and ever-increasing economic growth. Reverses are seen as temporary and as preparation for future improvements, much as a short economic recession within a multidecade period of economic growth.

This book, however, is animated by a different view. It recognizes that civilization is fragile, and that reverses can happen in years, or at most decades, that reshape human life, and often in a negative way.

There are points in history where, while the world's great civilizations seemed to be at the apex of their sophistication and power, their great achievements were lost in mere decades. The best example may be the Roman Empire, which in 300 CE stretched from England in the northwest to the Middle East in the southeast. By 500 CE the empire was falling apart. That new era has often been referred to as the Dark Ages precisely because Roman civilization, inherited from and influenced by the Greeks, was lost until the 1100s, when the Moslems of North Africa reintroduced classical ideas to Europe through Spain.

In the last one thousand years, Europe built a world based on Enlightenment ideas often influenced by the classics of the ancient world. As we think about the world, and specifically the United States, we can look at the twentieth century in this fashion, with periods of progress and regression. Through the Interwar period of the 1920s, the United States had been unsure of its role in the world, symbolized by the Senate's refusal in 1919 to ratify the Peace of Paris, which created the League of Nations designed to prevent another Great War (1914–1918).

World War II (1939–45) was the decisive revolutionary event for the United States, as it was for so many other countries. In 1939 the country was struggling to recover from the Great Depression—the worst, most prolonged, economic downturn it had ever seen. But by the end of 1945, and shortly thereafter, it was a different matter altogether. Along with the Soviet Union and the United Kingdom and its junior allies, the United States had vanquished fascism—the state powers of fascist Italy, Nazi Germany, and imperial Japan. The United States had the world's largest intact industrial structure; it controlled 80 percent of the world's gold supply; it was at full employment; and it was ready to take a leadership role in the world. The war set in motion internal transformations, particularly in the role of women, the place of African Americans and Hispanics, and the growth prospects of what would become known as a middle-class society. The United States and its allies supported the elaboration and ratification of the Geneva Conventions, which codified the proper treatment of prisoners of war (POWs). The world was moving away intellectually from the "might makes right" of power politics, and toward a new system with a single set of global rules for all states and other actors, regardless of their size and power. This was a step away from the "sovereign inequality"[8] of the nineteenth century, where imperial powers were free to attack the weak, and toward the concept of "sovereign equality" that we are now familiar with.

The Americans and the British led their allies in creating the United Nations (UN) and the Bretton Woods institutions, including the International Monetary Fund, and what would later be called the World Bank. With the Soviet Union nipping at their heels, those who designed these new institutions knew that the masses of the West would not accept a return to the deprivations of the Great Depression. During World War II they had been promised that governments and markets would create a better future. One of the many volumes of the *Collected Writings of John Maynard Keynes* starts with a letter written by Keynes in 1939 to the effect that people will not fight against fascism only to return to the Great Depression. They will, however, fight against it on a promise of a new and better world. The late 1940s and 1950s demonstrated a temporary reversal of these progressive pressures, as Rosie the Riveter was fired and sent home to bear children while her new husband, just demobilized from the military, took over her job.

Despite progress in racial integration of the US military, African Americans returned home to Jim Crow segregation in the South and elsewhere. And Senator Joe McCarthy got traction in the 1950s asking the question, "Who lost China?" after the Chinese Revolution. He claimed that the United States was being weakened by communists and communist sympathizers in the education system, the entertainment industry, and even the US Army. (The last accusation spelled the end of his influence.)

For twenty years beginning with the 1954 Supreme Court decision that "separation is inherently unequal" (*Brown v. Board of Education of Topeka, Kansas*), the United States moved progressively on race, gender, democratic participation, and equality. The civil rights movement ended legal discrimination throughout the country, and the role and consciousness of women were transformed, as were attitudes toward the environment, war and peace, and government. The Watergate scandal resulted in a president being brought down by an investigation into his own paranoid conspiracies against his enemies.

The 1970s was a time of great change. Congress reasserted itself, trying to put limits on executive power and, particularly, presidential war powers, as manifested in Vietnam. Democrats and Republicans came together in the US Senate to publicly issue a report exposing and arguing for an end to state-sponsored assassination. To undermine the possibility of a criminal statute, the Gerald Ford, Jimmy Carter, and Ronald Reagan administrations issued or modified executive orders against the planning and implementation of assassinations by US government employees. In the late 1970s President Carter gave the Panama Canal back to Panama, brokered a peace treaty between Israel and Egypt, made progress on arms control with the Soviet Union, and argued that human rights should be at the core of US foreign policy.

Though there were economic storm clouds on the horizon, by mid-decade economic equality within the United States was at a high point. There was progress on gender equality, race relations, and environmental protection. In retrospect, the New Deal bargain between the rich and poor, and labor and business, provided economic growth and relatively shared prosperity in the 1950s through the early 1970s. While it should not be romanticized, this economic situation can only be the envy of today's bottom 70 percent of Americans. The Equal Rights Amendment to the US Constitution had easily passed Congress and was deemed a shoo-in as protection for the rights of women in America. Optimists thought that the United States had finally turned the corner.

Even as the United States was starting to decline economically, a sign of the high-water mark in foreign policy was in the very existence and conclusions of the Church Committee. In an era of assassination and drone warfare, its interim report reads like a work from a very different time and place.[9] While not a radical document—it is, after all, an official report of a US Senate committee—in over 350 pages it describes the role of several administrations, the CIA, the military, and the State Department in planning, encouraging, or having advance knowledge of coups d'état and assassinations in Chile, the Congo, Cuba, the Dominican Republic, and Vietnam. Its revelations helped to burst the bubble of US assumptions of infallibility and devotion to high, unwavering principle. The committee is ultimately tentative in its conclusions, though it did recommend a statute that, were it on the books unamended, might render illegal much of the Bush and, especially, Obama policies on drone warfare and assassination. The bipartisan nature of the report is also notable. It was signed by Church and other Democratic luminaries such as Walter Mondale, Gary Hart, and Charles Mathias, Jr., but also by prominent Republicans of the day, including Howard Baker, John Tower, and the 1964 presidential nominee, Barry Goldwater.

Ronald Reagan took office in 1981, signaling the beginning of a rollback of all postwar achievements. Union rights would be curtailed, America would deindustrialize, income taxes for the rich would be cut numerous times, and the poor and the working class would sink back into greater poverty and insecurity. Steady, lifetime employment, possibly with a single enterprise, would come to be regarded as an unrealistic relic of a past economy. The Democratic Party would pass from the hands of the New Deal liberals, who remembered the problems of the world under *laissez-faire* capitalism, into the hands of the Democratic Leadership Council. This center-right group, represented by Bill and Hillary Clinton, and more recently Obama, carries the endorsement of Wall Street and other crisis-ridden "sunrise industries," including banking, insurance, and accounting and management services.

Despite the gainsaying and hyperpartisanship of the last fifteen years, Republicans must have known (and it has been borne out by events) that their high-income constituency was not too badly served by these new Democrats, whether in tax policy or in management of the US empire. While Jimmy Carter ended his time in 1980 with a military budget of around $80 billion, by 2015 it was over ten times that. As much as the United States is provoking China and Russia close to their own "spheres of influence," in reality it does not *yet* have a real superpower military rival. Perhaps this is why the US government is fighting multiple wars in Iraq, Afghanistan, Syria,[10] Yemen, and Pakistan, among others, and dealing with the havoc previously wreaked on countries such as Libya.

CHAPTER BY CHAPTER: THIS BOOK'S PLAN

The concern of this book is the frightening implications of drone warfare in the seemingly endless *global war on terrorism*. As an introduction to the pages that follow, we have established the historical background and raises the vital questions to be addressed in the rise of drones in military applications.

Chapter 1 focuses on the profound transformation underway in US strategic ambitions, as well as its overseas military activities. The rise of assassination and drone warfare is really only at the surface of these changes—perhaps the small part of the iceberg visible above the water line. There has not been enough public awareness or discussion of these developments and their medium- to long-term results. There is a certain irony that those who run the US government do so based on the pretense that they cut their teeth as critics of the old order and do things in a more enlightened fashion. The reality is far different.

In chapter 2 the roles of Congress, the judiciary, and especially the president, are examined. This involves questioning Bush- and Obama-era legal justifications for drone warfare, including the Obama development of the *kill list*. The idea of negative long-term consequences of the use of drones is introduced. Supreme Court decisions, such as *Hamdi v. Rumsfeld*, however, provide reason for optimism. Citizens must ask and answer the tough questions about the degree to which an imperial state requires ruthless tactics to survive.

The focus of chapter 3 is the background of the development of the military-industrial complex (MIC) in the United States, including a long history of providing misleading information on the costs and effectiveness of new weapons systems. The decline of some military-industrial product lines, such as contemporary fighter bombers, will be made up for by the rise of drone production and sales. Will the MIC prevent citizens from critical analysis of the long-term consequences of drone warfare?

Chapter 4 looks at the impact of drone warfare inside the US military, including the Taylorization and displacement of traditional cockpit pilots, the role of communications technology in increasing the role of senior officers making air-war combat decisions, and controversies among serving members and veterans regarding the "warrior status" of drone pilots. One of the under-discussed aspects of drone warfare is that it is finally a means to break the power of the pilots in the USAF. Debates over retention of drone pilots and their senior command potential are also considered, as is the controversy over the proposed awarding of a new military medal for drone warriors.

Chapter 5 features an analysis of the rush to develop drone technology for domestic use in the United States and ultimately globally. Military contractors want to develop civilian models of their technology for private sector firms and government to increase efficiency or cut costs. However, this may normalize it for domestic commercial and law-enforcement use, and overseas military use. It may also lead to domestic accidents and acts of terrorism. While there has been little public discussion, significant evidence already exists that the capabilities and reliability of domestic drone technology have been exaggerated.

In chapter 6 we tackle the role of experts, particularly think tanks. There has been an explosion in their number over the last thirty-five years, with a domination of conservative and capitalist libertarian ideas. The role of money and the donor's preferences are discussed, as is the possibility that think tanks are used by powerful people to produce ideas that may be novel, risky, or unpopular. Given changes in the mainstream media, including their need for free or cheap, digestible ideas, think tanks and canned expertise have risen greatly in visibility and influence on policy makers. The contemporary reality seems to be that most information for the general public comes from think tanks.

The topic of chapter 7 is the media, focusing on how lack of complete analysis in the mainstream media after 9/11 and in the run-up to, and then fallout of, the US invasions of Iraq and Afghanistan continue to plague the dialogue about drone warfare. Discussion will include media bias and ownership interests, reliance on official sources, lack of access for war reporting, the media's event orientation, persistence of unasked questions, lack of historical background, and labeling.

Chapter 8 examines resistance to drone warfare, including the view of practitioners and scholars of international law. The contemporary system of international law, despite the creation of fully autonomous drones, has potential in reducing or limiting drone use. Interestingly, those from outside the United States are far more likely to be critical of US use of weaponized drones. Simmering domestic resistance to drone warfare is in need of leadership. The international campaign to ban antipersonnel landmines is a good precedent, and useful case study, for how a movement might be organized.

Although introducing new material in a conclusion may be unorthodox, ours features a fascinating comparison between recent US activities in the

Middle East and those during the Vietnam War. With a particular analysis of the Phoenix program, we argue that recent activities in the Middle East are even more brazen and show less regard for the sovereignty of local governments, human rights, or the laws of war, than during the tragic Vietnam era.

NOTES

1. Josh Smith, "Drones Emerge from the Shadows to Become Key cog in U.S. War Machine," Reuters, June 7, 2016.

2. *United States Senate, Select Committee to Study Governmental Operations* (New York: W. W. Norton, 1976), xix.

3. Kevin McCaney, "A drone by any other name is . . . an RPA?" Defense Systems, May 23, 2014, http://defensesystems.com/articles/2014/05/23/dempsey-rpa-drones-uas.aspx

4. Brian Fung, "Why drone makers have declared war on the word 'drone,'" *Washington Post*, August 16, 2013, http://www.washingtonpost.com/blogs/the-switch/wp/2013/08/16/why-drone-makers-have-declared-war-on-the-word-drone/.

5. Chris Powell, "We Are Not Drones: Pilots, Sensor Operators Put Human Element in RPA Operations," *Airman*, October 21, 2013.

6. For a brief account of the breaking of the *Washington Post* pressmen in 1975–1977, see Cal Winslow, "Overview: The Rebellion from Below," in *Rebel Rank and File: Labor militancy and revolt from below in the long 1970s*, eds.A. Brenner, R. Brenner, and C. Winslow (London and New York: Verso, 2010), 1–36.

7. Grégoire Chamayou, *A Theory of the Drone* (New York and London: The New Press, 2015), 99.

8. David Chandler, *From Kosovo to Kabul: Human Rights and International Intervention* (London and Sterling, VA: Pluto Press, 2002).

9. Church Report, see note 2 above.

10. Greg Miller, "U.S. launches secret drone campaign to hunt Islamic State leaders in Syria," *Washington Post*, September 1, 2015, https://www.washingtonpost.com/world/national-security/us-launches-secret-drone-campaign-to-hunt-islamic-state-leaders-in-syria/2015/09/01/723b3e04–5033–11e5–933e-7d06c647a395_story.html.

Chapter One

Shifts in American War Policy

It is fitting in a work on the rise of assassination and drone warfare to examine the conventional wisdom of US military policy and its relationship to international and domestic law. Armed conflict is nothing new, so putting this discussion into a historical perspective is helpful—with a brief look at wars through history, and how wars and beliefs about them have changed over time. It's particularly interesting to consider the Augustinian view of war as just, because it meant those who did wrong were punished. In the sixteenth and seventeenth centuries, there was a move away from this punitive view; it was a time when soldiers followed the rules of war and did so without question. And because they were following orders, guilt or blame was not expected to be an issue. More than one observer has noted a return to both of these modes of thinking in recent US military policy.

Also in this chapter is a discussion of the law-enforcement perspective on international conflicts, and of international humanitarian law (IHL), established as a set of rules that seeks to limit the effects of armed conflict. The case study of Canadian child soldier Omar Khadr will prove to be useful. There is discussion about the need for a transformation in how we conduct warfare because of where we are today. For instance, following the Cold War between the United States and the Soviet Union, changes in war strategy and technology have meant that far more civilians have died than soldiers.

The immediate US response to 9/11 and the resulting wars are examined here. What were the options of the US government and why were some of them so quickly dismissed? Why was the United States so seemingly anxious to engage in war? How has history provided lessons on a better way to proceed? The current track the US government is on, especially since it includes drone warfare, is a dangerous one.

A BRIEF HISTORY OF WAR

While anthropologists have identified small-scale societies in which people have lived peaceably with each other and their neighbors, even a casual survey of the last three thousand years indicates widespread armed conflict with often brutal consequences for civilians. In the ancient world it was not unusual for the victor to kill the men and enslave the women and children. Empires expanded their boundaries by force if necessary, until opponents possessed even greater force. For most of the past five hundred years in Europe, widespread civilian death in war has been more common than efforts to prevent harm to noncombatants. With unprecedented technology, such as high explosives, repeating rifles, machine guns, and airplanes, the mass slaughters continue—much as in the American Civil War, the Great War (World War I), World War II, and in the "limited" wars since.

The twentieth century was different, however, in the way that World War II represented a tipping point against the continuation of the old order. By 1945 even the great powers and superpowers were so traumatized by total war that they agreed to a series of changes to the world's organization that could restrict their own room to maneuver. They wrote a charter for a new entity, the UN. It essentially outlawed war as a policy choice, with the exception of self-defense when the global community neglected to come to a state's aid. They developed a Security Council based on the nineteenth-century Concert of Europe system in which the five allied and victorious powers were expected to "act in concert" to jointly manage the global security system.

Leaders in the late 1940s and early 1950s also seemed to accept the view that Karl Polanyi expressed in 1944 that absolute faith in the "gold standard" and the self-correcting market economy were utopian ideas. The future would require global efforts to aid development and reconstruction, and state leadership. (Numerous commentators have noted that by contemporary Republican Party standards, President Dwight D. Eisenhower [1953–1961] could be labeled a socialist. President Richard Nixon [1969–1974] could be a liberal—albeit a much-hated one.) In the late 1940s, the surviving senior Nazi leadership was tried for *crimes against humanity* at Nuremberg, and the Geneva Conventions on the proper conduct of combatants were extended and elaborated. At the same time, the principle of *national self-determination* was affirmed, recognizing oppressed people's right to struggle against imperial powers that denied their independence.

At the base of these postwar legal and moral developments was the belief that when war occurred between two or more states, IHL must be applied. A separate body of law known as "human rights law" also addressed non-international conflict situations. Both practically and philosophically, by the mid-twentieth century, attitudes toward war and combat had changed. In the

Christian tradition, starting with St. Augustine of Hippo (354–430 CE) and elaborated by St. Thomas Aquinas (1225–1274 CE) and others, killing in war was just because the true Christian prevented evildoers from committing further sin. As Helen M. Kinsella points out, the Augustinian tradition was not designed to prevent Christian engagement in war, but rather to legitimize it.[1] To kill in war was to do God's work. More than one commentator has noted the implicit return of this thinking by the George W. Bush administration (2001–2009) during the global war on terrorism. And Reagan's labeling of the Soviet Union as an "evil empire" can now be seen as a precursor of this, for prior to the 1980s, administrations engaged in more sober and businesslike management of the power relationship between NATO and the Warsaw Pact alliances. One need only think of Henry Kissinger, national security advisor and secretary of state in the Nixon and Ford administrations. In contrast to the Augustinian view, the dominant rationale for both deterrence and proxy wars during the Cold War (1948–1990) was that the United States was responding to threats, attacks, or probes by the Soviet Union and its allies. It was not "personal" in that the relationship was viewed through the lenses of diplomatic conduct, the wisdom of history, and power politics.

As Colin McKeough notes, the great achievement in thinking about war in the sixteenth and seventeenth centuries, by legal minds like Vattel and later Grotius, was to move away from the punitive approach that dominated the Christian tradition for a thousand years.[2] As part of the Enlightenment, or early modern period, international-law thinkers noted that the rise of sovereignty meant that soldiers were instruments of their sovereign leaders. So long as soldiers followed the rules of war, they were not guilty. Soldiers under any command, including insurgent groups, do not bear the same level of responsibility as their highest commander. In other words, they are not common criminals. Remarkable the degree to which the 1500-year-old Augustinian perspective has so prominently snuck back into the Western approaches to the wars in the Middle East. When a US helicopter was shot down in Afghanistan with the loss of many Navy SEALs, the government response, now almost reflexive, was that the "guilty parties will be found and punished."

JUST WAR

The Augustinian perspective is further illustrated by the case of Omar Khadr, the Canadian child soldier. Khadr was born in Toronto in September 1986 to an unsavory family with loyalty to the anti-Western Afghani Taliban and a close connection to Osama bin Laden and al Qaeda. For most of his first nine years he was raised in Pakistan, but by 1996 ended up in Afghanistan, living for a time in the bin Laden compound. From the age of ten he was given weapons-training by his family, like many rural North Americans. On July 22, 2002, during the US occupation of Afghanistan, Khadr was apprehended for throwing a hand grenade, killing one US soldier, Christopher Speer, and injuring another. Although only fifteen, he was not treated as a prisoner of war or as a child soldier. He was also not considered a juvenile or "young offender" (to use Canadian terminology).

At sixteen Khadr was transferred to Camp X-Ray in Guantanamo Bay, Cuba, where, in October 2002 and in February 2003, members of the Royal Canadian Mounted Police and the Canadian Security and Intelligence Service interviewed him. They turned over information to the US military. There were significant legal machinations in the following seven years, including in Canadian courts. In October 2010, he accepted a plea bargain, admitting guilt to five crimes, including murder, in exchange for a sentence of no more than eight years. In April 2012, US Defense secretary Leon Panetta signed off on Khadr's transfer to the Canadian judicial system, and by mid-2015 Khadr was out on parole, living with his lawyer in Edmonton, Alberta. The Canadian courts modified his parole conditions to provide him with greater freedom. [3]

It is remarkable that Khadr was treated as a murderer rather than a child soldier, that he and his family were sued in a US civil court, and that the civil jury awarded the Speer family millions in a wrongful death judgment. In liberal circles the Iraqi War is more likely to be seen as a US act of aggression than the invasion of Afghanistan in the fall of 2001. But many Afghanis, as well as the Khadr family, saw the United States as an aggressor. They considered themselves a resistance army.

One of the problems of the Augustinian view of war, and our return to it, is that no effort is made to see the conflict from the other side. When the United Kingdom and Argentina fought each other in the Falklands War, both sides knew the other's point of view and did not characterize the other as evil to the same degree as we find in these Afghani and Iraqi cases. An extreme version of our mental devolution is found in the story of William C. Bradford, who started work as a professor at the US Military Academy at West Point, New York, in the summer of 2015. He had just published a paper in which he argued that it was legitimate for the US military to target and kill legal scholars who criticize the US war on terrorism. According to Bradford, they can be targeted at work and home, and in media outlets that interview them. [4] He also advocated attacks of Islamic holy sites. Shortly after public fuss over this article, his past writing, and allegations that he inflated his credentials, Bradford resigned from West Point. One has to wonder, however, why he was hired in the first place.

This has happened against a background of a transformation of the country in the forty or fifty years beginning with World War II. As Garry Wills argues in his fascinating account, the US political system had the potential to be a functioning republic in form and reality, with its large number of elected offices and its separation and sharing of powers. This ended with developing the atomic bomb in 1945 and succumbing to the temptation to project its power over an ever-increasing portion of the globe. Because the atomic bomb can only be deployed by one person (or a committee acting as a single agent), it elevated the presidency to a paramount position. Congress could only be reactive as the power to *declare* war declined in the wake of in-creased power to *make* war. The United States made the transition from a small, agrarian republic to a "national security state," one that is unrespon-sive to public opinion, just as one would expect as republican ideals fade. Wills identifies twenty-five events in peacetime, from October 1948 through November 1952, that effectively set the United States on its current course. The changes since 9/11 are just a deepening of these trends.[5]

Christopher Fuller argues that the current drone war and the Bush-Obama enthusiasm for assassination is a revival of directions pioneered in the Rea-gan administration.[6] He cites a rather obscure National Security Decision Directive (no. 138),[7] entitled *Combating Terrorism*, with the following key passage: that the CIA director will pursue "lawful measures to:

- Increase cooperation with the security agencies of other friendly govern-ments.
- Unilaterally and/or in concert with other countries *neutralize* or counter terrorist organizations and terrorist leaders.
- Develop an information exploitation program, aimed at disrupting and demoralizing terrorist groups." (emphasis added)

Some theorize that use of the term *neutralize* legitimizes assassination. As we will see when we discuss the Phoenix program later, however, the term is understood to "render neutral" rather than terminate. In any event, there is no disputing that for a long time the United States has violated the sovereignty of other countries with covert operations against individuals. Two major changes since the Reagan period have been to abandon the insistence on "lawful measures" and to extend permanent war to a truly global battlefield.

Of course the Obama administration and US military can treat users of the surface-to-air missile as common criminals if they like, but the United States invaded Afghanistan on flimsy grounds and has been the *de facto* occupying power, along with its allies, ever since. So is there any surprise that a resis-tance attacks? The timing of the return to the Augustinian view of war is not a coincidence, because it is designed for a situation in which a Christian force faces an unknown and mysterious adversary in battle. This could be the peoples of the New World, the Ottoman Turks in the sixteenth century on-ward, or those of the Islamic world today, primarily in the Middle East. Is there any doubt that countries that are predominantly Christian, or at least with overwhelmingly Christian governments, waging war against predominantly Islamic countries and movements have contributed to this revival of the Augustinian perspective? Or perhaps the revival has enabled new forms of warfare launched by the Christian West?

END OF JUST-WAR TRADITION

In the twentieth century, the just-war tradition within IHL departed from this older tradition in virtually every major aspect. Recourse to war is not legal under the UN Charter unless it is defensive and truly the last resort, in which case there are elaborate rules. In contrast to the ancient Christian tradition, war is a policy decision of governments for which individual soldiers, sailors, and air crew are not morally responsible. Combatants are considered "privileged" when they wear their country's uniform, carry arms openly, and are under responsible command. Civilians are not to be harmed; only members of the opponent's military are subject to attack. Whereas twentieth-century international law focused on the long-term relationships between and among nations and states, drone warfare and these new policies focus only on the short term—until the next election.

One of the principles of the twentieth-century revision of IHL is *noncombatant immunity*, the idea that warfare is conducted between armed and uniformed combatants only. Kinsella makes a valid point in saying that there is much more doubt in the civilian-combatant distinction then we normally recognize, but it is helpful that the tradition also says that when there is doubt, "that person shall be considered to be a civilian."[8] The discussion speaks to the importance of getting it right on the decision to go to war, for who among us can say that wars always go as planned or that anyone is really in total control of either their conduct or outcome? As John Tirman writes in his fascinating book on US attitudes toward civilian deaths in war, one presumably unintended shift is that the ratio of soldiers-to-civilians killed has flipped from 9:1 in World War I to 1:9 beginning with the ethnic wars in the post–Cold War era in the 1990s.[9] In an age of assassination and extrajudicial execution, civilian immunity as a principle is replaced by what academic Igor Primoratz refers to ironically as *combatant immunity*.[10] The CIA runs drone strikes, a clear violation of the rules of war because the agents are not uniformed soldiers. But even those in uniform, in bases in the United States, Germany, Saudi Arabia, and other countries, are effectively immune from harm even as they rain death down on militants and civilians. The world has been turned upside down. Ian Shaw and Majed Akhter[11] put it well:

> Contemporary targeted killings take place against a background defined by a blurring of the categories of war, solder and military, on the one hand, and peace, criminal and police, on the other. The figure of the terrorist increasingly

straddled these two classifications: not quite "enemy combatant" and not quite "criminal."

In the translation of his recent book[12] Grégoire Chamayou arrives at many of the same insights, but not through the just-war tradition or twentieth-century international law. Much of his work is about the transformation of modern warfare. He notes that historically war had the structure of the duel, with two self-aware and willing participants, whereas now it has become hide-and-seek. The use of remote killing machines like drones invites charges of cowardice. There is now something pre-sovereign and neofeudal because the drone power presumes to have the "right of pursuit" to find targeted individuals regardless of lines written on maps. Soldiering is no longer about self-sacrifice, but rather self-preservation. Since this new war is seemingly without risk, the practitioners must rely on the doctrine of assassination, while the targets lack any access to self-defense. Along the same lines, Shaw and Akhter suggest, "What we find significant in today's drone 'man hunt' is that the Hobbesian state of nature—of violence targeted against the individual—has returned as a central organizing principle."[13]

The legitimate goal of the now-fading Enlightenment theory of war is to *defeat* the enemy, not to kill enemy combatants or civilians. It should also be noted that it is widely accepted that force is only legitimate to achieve the political end of victory, not to exact revenge upon the opposing military or civilians. A military is legally obliged to provide quarter to, and take as POWs, any opposing combatant who surrenders. This last point has particular importance, because it provides *de facto* defeated troops the option of safety in surrender rather than killing and fighting to the death. This works philosophically and practically for both winners and losers. POWs are entitled to be properly fed and sheltered, not to be subject to torture or rough treatment, or to be forced to work for their captors. When one side follows these rules it provides a reciprocal incentive for the other side to do so as well.[14]

LAW-ENFORCEMENT OPTIONS AND HUMAN RIGHTS

With the end of the Cold War and the Soviet collapse at the end of the 1980s, observers of modern warfare have argued that we were witnessing a transformation in war, either as the development of "new wars" or a "revolution in military affairs."[15] They argued that civil wars would become more common than inter-state wars, as societies fell apart once the side-supports provided by the United States and Soviet Union were removed. Further, ethnic conflict would emerge after having been suppressed by the competition of Enlightenment ideologies like liberalism and socialism, or communism and capitalism. One of the concerns of the United States and other established powers over the last twenty years was that this would be an era of "asymmetric conflict," in which they would be challenged to win the struggle against much weaker but more focused and committed opponents. Despite its enormous power, the United States lacked ultimate success in the Korean Conflict (1950–1953), and particularly in Vietnam (1965–1975) under these conditions.

This was of particular concern as the country continually expanded its own global definition of its vital interests. In the 1950s and 1960s the United States overthrew governments or interfered in countries in Latin America, but also in Iran, Lebanon, Iraq, and elsewhere. By the late 1970s, the Carter administration was defining the Persian Gulf as an area of vital interest, and was funding and training "anti-modernist" Islamist fighters in Afghanistan and Pakistan to provoke a Soviet entry into "their Vietnam." This eventually happened in December 1979. The Soviets were bogged down in Afghanistan for much of ten years but as Carter's national security advisor Zbigniew Bzrezinski admitted in a widely noted interview much later, he thought bringing down the Soviet empire was worth the risk of the creation and encouragement of the fundamentalist Islamic militants in that part of the world.[16]

In the 1990s and 2000s, in an era of supposed democratization, the United States found itself increasingly aligned with the authoritarian and undemocratic Saudi Arabia, Kuwait, Bahrain, and other Gulf states, because of economics, strategy, self-interest, and fossil-fuel energy. The desire to alternatively defend and control these royalist friends enraged those who had brought down the Soviet Union, particularly the *Mujahadeen*. In the 1990s the United States faced attacks from these forces on their embassies and the navy ship the USS *Cole*, as well as the first effort to blow up the World Trade Center in New York.

But the attack on the World Trade Center and the Pentagon on September 11, 2001, attributed to bin Laden's al Qaeda organization, put the US government to the test. Would the president and Congress view this as an act of war, the first shot in a prolonged conflict, and respond as such? Or would they see it as President Clinton saw the first effort to attack the World Trade Center, as essentially a crime to be addressed through law enforcement? The advantage of these two choices is their clarity. If it is an act of war, then once one identifies the state responsible, the victim declares war on that state, defeats it, and signs a treaty to end the conflict. Apart from the *initial* loss of life, 9/11 did not have the military significance of the 1941 Pearl Harbor attack, which was a crippling blow to the US military in the Pacific by the Japanese, then one of the world's great military powers. And Afghanistan (commonly held responsible for al Qaeda) was certainly no imperial Japan. A conventional war with Afghanistan would yield an easy victory for the United States, similar to those in Grenada and Panama years before. After 9/11 the

United States had overwhelming world sympathy and it could have defeated Afghanistan following the rules of war from IHL.

Of course, the US government could also have pursued with vigor the law-enforcement route, in cooperation with most of the world's states. They would have treated the al Qaeda hijackers and their supporters as criminals, using police and judicial means of seeking redress. The United States invaded Afghanistan on the pretense that its Taliban government refused to extradite bin Laden and other key al Qaeda personnel. It could have implemented sanctions against a country harboring these fugitives, waiting as long as necessary for them to be turned over. A country as powerful as the United States would not have been denied had it used its overwhelming power and treasure to achieve such a small task. Pursuing the law-enforcement perspective would have allowed the United States to protect the human rights of all involved—something clearly not done in the fifteen years since 9/11. With the permission of the state involved, suspects could have been arrested, transported, and tried in US federal court, and if found guilty, punished in accordance with US law. (Admittedly, the defendants would have used their trial to expose US involvement in their organization's creation in the 1980s; only advocates of US and Western *realpolitik*, not law enforcement or truth seekers, would suppress that defense.) These were crimes committed in the United States in violation of US laws. It was well known that al Qaeda was a small organization that could have been broken through pressure and apprehensions. Choosing law enforcement allows the country that is not eager for war to avoid it. But in 2001, avoiding war was not a high priority for the Bush administration and congressional establishment, both Republican and Democrat. In retrospect, and as some identified at the time,[17] it would have been a much more effective way to respond.

GLOBAL WAR ON TERRORISM

Ironically, the US government did the worst thing it could do under the circumstances. It avoided picking one of two clear options and instead chose a third, hybrid option that provided maximum flexibility, but also maximum risk of military and intellectual calamity. The Bush administration, with congressional support, launched its war on terrorism. Tactics that the government occasionally employed in the past—pre-emptive invasion, killing civilians, and summary execution and torture—became commonplace, official policy. This war, rather than focusing on limited goals in one or two states, was much more ambitious. Policy makers including Donald Rumsfeld and Dick Cheney soon admitted it might go on for decades. Because it was a war on tactics (and those adversaries who use and support them), the administration was quick to personalize it. This was a virtual invitation for the US military, mercenaries like Blackwater, the CIA, and aligned militaries, to treat these people as less than human once they were captured. They would deny them the privileges of either the POW or noncombatant status.

The Bush administration lawyers tried to do legal somersaults to define the captured as "illegal combatants," to claim that Guantanamo Bay's Camp X-Ray, where detainees were kept, was *not* the equivalent of US soil (perhaps a surprise to the Cubans) and therefore out of reach of federal courts. It was legal to claim "extraordinary rendition" of the captured to countries like Syria, where it was known they would be tortured. (By 2013, Bashir Al Assad, the dictator of Syria, faced an armed insurgency supported by the West. Like Moammar Qaddafi a year before him, he must have wondered, "Where's the loyalty?") Further, Bush and Obama lawyers claimed that it is acceptable for the US government, based on presidential order alone, to run a series of "black site" secret prisons in Iraq, Afghanistan, central Europe, the island of Diego Garcia, and many other locations.

By choosing to fall between two stools (the inter-state-war and law-enforcement perspectives), the Bush administration bequeathed the worst of both to the world. It, followed by Obama, chose a course of action that conveniently made it possible to render moot the rules that had been achieved in the twentieth century. In the netherworld of the global war on terrorism, why not invade countries like Afghanistan, Iraq, Pakistan, Yemen, and Libya at will? (North Korea and Iran, the other two members of Bush's "axis of evil" in addition to Iraq, would be spared only because things went so badly from 2001–2004.) Also, why not target urban infrastructure like water systems, medical facilities, and electrical grids? Or why not kill civilians on a large scale or use extraordinary rendition to send captives to Syria, Libya, and other authoritarian states to be tortured? Why not legitimize water-boarding as an acceptable form of "aggressive interrogation technique," or allow and encourage unspeakable acts at the Abu Graib prison in Iraq? Once they located bin Laden in 2011, instead of arresting and trying him, they killed him and dumped his body at sea, denying his family the right to bury their wayward son consistent with their religious traditions. With no due process and no coroner's death certificate, the Obama administration then wondered why people asked whether they had really gotten their man. The country did not exactly attract the global trust and sympathy as in the months after 9/11.

The United States elevated a relatively unimportant individual and movement to global prominence. After the disputed election of November 2000, the attacks on 9/11 saved the presidency of George W. Bush from ineffectiveness and irrelevance. The US reaction to the attacks must have been exactly what bin Laden was hoping for. By starting the war on terrorism, primarily against bin Laden, the United States was essentially conferring on him *de facto* statehood that he and his movement did not warrant. If we are to take their efforts at face value, the Bush administration made one of the greatest mistakes a superpower can make: it elevated a much weaker adversary to equivalence. The greatest help to the radical is the notoriety, and some might say legitimacy, that the superpower's attention confers. The United States and its allies were unfettered by either the IHL of the rules of war or international human rights associated with the law-enforcement perspective. They angered large numbers of citizens in the countries that they bombed and invaded. For the families of the hundreds of thousands of Moslems that they killed in the last dozen years, many of them civilians, what could be more logical than joining the local franchise of al Qaeda? Intellectual error has become fulfilled prediction. Widespread attacks in the Middle East were premised on perceived widespread enmity toward the United States. They in fact created the widespread enmity.

It is ironic that by July 2013 the US military and government were accepting this logic when they faced reporters who asked, "Who are these 'associated forces' that we are at war with, in addition to al Qaeda and the Taliban?" The answer, from Lt. Col. Jim Gregory, was that the list is classified "because elements that might be considered 'associated forces' can build credibility by being listed as such by the United States. . . . We cannot afford to inflate these organizations that rely on violent extremist ideology to strengthen their ranks."[18]

It was Bush who, in an unguarded moment, referred to the war on terrorism as a "crusade," and many Westerners, academics, and policy makers, have followed Samuel Huntington in referring to a "clash of civilizations." Perhaps it is audiences in the Middle East who have been most easily convinced that this is the real state of relations with the West. Surely enough, and predictably, the invasions and firepower have created more new recruits than bin Laden could ever have dreamed of. Countries such as Egypt, Pakistan, and Yemen are now more unstable than in 2001. Libya has totally fallen apart, the evidence visible every day in European ports of entry. Despite the Bush administration's stated enthusiasm for a "democratic wave" to sweep over the Middle East, the United States has been doing its best, in light of the Arab Spring of 2011, to protect selected allied governments, including Israel, Bahrain, Saudi Arabia, Kuwait, and Yemen. Even in Egypt, where a democratic wave exists, the predictable result is of adversaries of the Western world coming into power. The best the United States and its allies can hope for is to declare victory, go home, and take their embedded media with them. They should cross their fingers that with the passage of time no one at home will notice as the countries once lavished with so much attention now fall apart.

CONCLUSION

What are just and unjust wars? How has drone warfare changed the game? Bush's leap into a military solution after 9/11 set the stage for continuing conflicts in many countries. In this chapter we have shown that through most of its history the United States functioned along with other countries in a global system in which there was at least a rhetorical acceptance of the modern version of international law and ethics in warfare. Over the last number of decades, and especially since the collapse of the Soviet Union in 1990 and then 9/11 in 2001, the United States has made both a rhetorical and practical commitment to unilateralism and a rewritten version of the conduct of states in the use of violence. In reacting to 9/11 the United States did not apply either the law-enforcement perspective or an inter-state-war perspective, but rather a mishmash of the two. The enemy was personalized and members of the US military and "private contractors" were allowed, even encouraged, to react with anger. The demonizing of the enemy has led to the use of harsh and hard-hearted measures, such as torture, terrorizing, and killing of civilians, and the attack on civilian infrastructure. In the past, only evil enemies would have pursued these methods. The rise of drone warfare is a continuation and extension of the willingness to employ assassination and these harsh techniques used in Afghanistan, Iraq, and now other countries.

NOTES

1. Helen Kinsella, *The Image before the Weapon: A Critical History of the Distinction between Combatant and Civilian* (Ithaca and London: Cornell University Press, 2011), 34.

2. Colm McKeough, "Civilian Immunity in War: Augustine to Vattel," in *Civilian Immunity in War*, edited by Igor Primoratz, (Oxford: Oxford University Press, 2007), 62–83.

3. Canadian Press, "Omar Khadr timeline," *Toronto Star*, April 24, 2015, http://www.thestar.com/news/world/2015/04/24/omar-khadr-timeline.html.

4. Spencer Ackerman, "West Point professor calls on US military to target legal critics of war on terror," *The Guardian*, August 29, 2015, http://www.theguardian.com/us-news/2015/aug/29/west-point-professor-target-legal-critics-war-on-terror?CMP=share_btn_tw.

5. Garry Wills, *Bomb Power: The Modern Presidency and the National Security State* (New York: The Penguin Press, 2010).

6. Christopher Fuller, "The Eagle Comes Home to Roost: The Historical Origins of the CIA's Lethal Drone Program." *Intelligence and National Security*, 2014. DOI: 10.1080/02684527.2014.895569.

7. White House, NSDD 138, April 4, 1984, 4, http://www.reagan.utexas.edu/archives/reference/Scanned%20NSDDS/NSDD138.pdf.

8. Kinsella, *The Image*, 5.

9. John Tirman, *The Deaths of Others: The Fate of Civilians in America's Wars* (Oxford and New York: Oxford University Press, 2011), 4.

10. Igor Primoratz, *Civilian Immunity*, 4. See note 2 above.

11. Ian Shaw and M. Akhter, "The Dronification of State Violence," *Critical Asian Studies* 46(2 [2014]): 211–34. DOI: 10.1080/14672715.2014.898452.

12. Chamayou, *A Theory of the Drone* (New York and London: The New Press, 2015), 17, 34, 53, 101, 157.

13. Shaw and Akhter, "Dronification of State Violence," 230.

14. The literature on IHL is voluminous, but in this section we rely mostly on P. Alston and E. MacDonald, eds., *Human Rights, Intervention and the Use of Force*; M. Byers, *War Law*; N. Melzer, *Targeted Killing in International Law*, and; H. Steiner, P. Alston, and R. Goodman, *International Human Rights in Context*.

15. Mary Kaldor, *New and Old Wars: Organized Violence in a Global Era* (Stanford, CA: Stanford University Press, 1999). Martin Shaw, *The New Western Way of War: Risk-Transfer Qar and Its Crisis in Iraq* (Cambridge, UK, and Malden, MA: Polity Press, 2005).

16. Betty Glad, *An Outsider in the White House: Jimmy Carter, His Advisors and the Making of American Foreign Policy* (Ithaca, NY: Cornell University Press, 2009). Chalmers Johnson, *Blowback: The Costs and Consequences of American Empire*, 2nd ed. (New York: Holt Paperbacks, 2004).

17. There is much discussion in *Z Magazine* and other outlets in 2001–2003 regarding alternatives to US invasion of Afghanistan and Iraq, and advocating a law-enforcement reaction to 9/11.

18. Cora Currier, "Who Are We at War With? That's Classified," *ProPublica*, July 26, 2013, http://www.propublica.org/article/who-are-we-at-war-with-thats-classified.

Chapter Two

Government's Role in Drone Warfare

The election of Barack Obama in 2009 created an expectation throughout the world for real political and economic transformation. Many expected change from the new bipartisan foreign- and military-policy consensus. But clearly, rather than policy transformation by the US government, there has been an entrenchment and continuation of established policy. This should not come as a surprise. There is no reason to believe that transformation was even the intention of the man himself or those powerful people around him. As G. William Domhoff has written, "President Obama's network of donors was similar to those of most of the successful national-level candidates in that it built on wealthy contributors from growth coalitions on up to the corporate community."[1] There is no better example of policy continuity and deepening than the subject matter of this book.

Candidate Obama criticized US detention practices in the George W. Bush era, but once in power his own approach was "kill, not capture," which allowed him to avoid the dilemma of what to do with the captured. He succeeded in a feat of Clinton-style "triangulation," developing a value-free-policy position to minimize opposition and maximize support. Obama said he would get out of Iraq but beef up US efforts in Afghanistan, allowing him to reassure militarists that his would not be a pacifist presidency. The expansion of assassination, and what has turned out to be more random killing, was never mentioned during the campaign, nor was the need to open new fronts in a growing list including Pakistan, Libya, Somalia, and Yemen. Perhaps he was not counting on the fact that in 2008 the last of the blowback and fallout from US military and foreign policies in the Middle East was yet to be seen.

In 2016, the United States finds itself embroiled in a region-wide civil war, with fluid sides and fronts in Afghanistan, Iraq, Yemen, Syria, Pakistan, Libya, Saudi Arabia, and elsewhere. Given the war-weariness of the

American people and a sense that these efforts are pointless and expensive in blood and treasure, it is unlikely that the principal US response will be ground troops. Enter the rise of drone warfare, the new form of warfare that would allegedly allow the precise targeting of key figures in the leadership of terrorist movements hostile to the United States and its Middle East friends, as well as suspicious but otherwise unknown people. This great increase in the use of drones, beyond anything the previous Bush administration could have imagined, has allegedly allowed for the degradation of al Qaeda, the Islamic State (*Da'ish*), and other adversaries, and at an acceptable political and economic cost.

This chapter will cover the rise of drone warfare in assassination, the Obama administration's legal rationale for this shift, the institution of the kill list in the hands of the president, and also the broad question of the constitutionality of this new form of warfare.

THE RISE OF DRONE WARFARE AS MEANS OF ASSASSINATION

It is fair to say that one of the more surprising aspects of the Obama administration has been its embrace of assassination via weaponized drones. Drones were developed in the United States in the 1930s and 1940s, particularly for military target practice. They were used in a limited way during Vietnam, but their application exploded in the 1990s, pioneered by Israel in the Occupied Territories. Under the George W. Bush administration, they were initially used for reconnaissance, with only forty-five strikes over eight years. In the first year of the Obama administration there were fifty-one reported uses of drones in Pakistan alone, and another 118 there the next year.[2] In 2012, the Obama administration opened up a new front with forty-six drone strikes in Yemen.[3] This trend has continued and accelerated over the eight years of the Obama presidency.

Internal rationales for the new US tactics were not exclusive to the Bush era but obviously have also been largely adopted by the Obama administration. In an April 2012 speech at the Woodrow Wilson Center in Washington, DC,[4] John Brennan, assistant to the president for homeland security and counterterrorism, and later Director of the CIA, first admitted publicly that the United States does kill militants and terrorists using drone attacks and other means. As a long-time senior CIA official, Brennan served George Tenet in the era of "extraordinary rendition," waterboarding, secret prisons, manipulated intelligence, and illegal, warrantless wiretapping. Deemed too controversial to be the choice for CIA director in Obama's first term, Brennan was hired into the White House instead. Brennan's perspective is a rosy one, in which these actions are justified by congressional resolution and are consistent with US law, Constitution, and the right of self-defense. His reading of the Constitution is very much like that of the Bush administration—it has provided a president-centered politics in which the president commands the military and can, without restraint, use the military and intelligence assets as the president sees fit. In his account, with rare exceptions, only militants and terrorists are killed. The United States only intervenes with the host government's permission, or when that government cannot or will not apprehend or neutralize the subject. According to Brennan, US adversaries are becoming weaker all the time, and the drone attacks meet the traditional tests of necessity, proportionality, and humanity.

The hardest case to make is that not only is the Obama drone war legal and appropriate, but that it is also legal and appropriate for the Obama administration to kill US citizens at home or abroad. This comes from a law professor at the University of St. Thomas School of Law, Michael Stokes Paulsen. In a stark but fascinating argument, based on a presentation before the conservative Federalist Society, Professor Paulsen takes the most assertive position in justification for Obama administration policies. Lest he be thought a shill for the administration, he stated in 2013 that the United States has, "an exceedingly poor Commander in Chief serving in the office of the President . . . , arguably the weakest such commander in more than 100 years."[5] To sum up his central argument, Paulsen states that "in his capacity as military Commander in Chief of the national armed forces in time of constitutionally authorized war, [the President] has the plenary power and discretion under the US Constitution to target and kill specific individuals that he in good faith determines to be active enemy combatants engaged in lawful or unlawful hostilities against the United States." This can include US citizens. To get there, Paulsen argues that: 1) the Authorization for Use of Military Force (AUMF) of September 18, 2011, remains a legally operative authorization of war; 2) Anwar al-Awlaki, the US citizen killed by a drone strike, was a legitimate target; 3) the president is empowered to judge that the victim was a legitimate target of war; 4) based on precedents going back to the US Civil War, his citizenship is of no relevance; 5) there is no "due process of war" that can restrain the president; and 6) international law is only a political and diplomatic constraint on the United States, not a domestic constraint.[6]

Paulsen can take these positions because he accepts as true all the claims made by the government even though they are not verified by a third party. He accepts that the AUMF has universal application in both space and time, though admittedly its drafting is overbroad; that the United States is correct or has told the truth about the crimes or activities of Anwar al-Awlaki; that in a dubious state of war, the US Bill of Rights does not apply to American citizens outside the country (even though the right to due process is also broadly written and can be argued to apply to noncitizens); and that there are no domestic or international legal constraints on the presidential conduct of war.

The key document about the Obama administration's specific justification for both its assassination program and the inclusion of a US citizen in that program was authored by David J. Barron, acting assistant attorney general, and released to the public by federal court order in April 2014.[7] In the document, one-third to 40 percent of which is redacted, Barron begins by establishing that governments cannot kill or murder except based on the "public authority justification." Further, existing federal criminal law makes it illegal for one US citizen to kill another outside the United States (18 USC 1119, "Foreign Murder of United States Nationals"). Barron then goes on to say that the "lawful conduct of war" is an example of a public authority justification for killing, and that in the case of al-Awlaki the test is met. If Barron's information is correct, al-Awlaki as senior commander of an al Qaeda-affiliated organization is associated closely enough to the 9/11 attackers to make him a legitimate target. It is fair, according to Barron, to say that he is planning imminent attacks as there is no reason to think that he has stood down or is *hors de combat* (out of combat). Consequently al-Awlaki's US citizenship does not come into play.

Barron claims that the United States is in a "non-international armed conflict" with al Qaeda, albeit one that does spill across borders. In contrast to an "international conflict" (or more accurately an "inter-state conflict"), it is less restrained by international law because its normal form is a civil war within one or two countries. (The conflict in Vietnam was treated by the Vietnamese, if not by the United States, as a non-international conflict.) Perhaps for this reason Barron also seems untroubled by the fact that the CIA carries out drone strikes, or, as we now know, issues strike orders to the "contractor," the US military. In the law of war, combatants must be in military uniform, must carry their weapons openly and be under responsible command. It is a war crime for CIA officers to engage in inter-state war, though perhaps in the view of the Obama administration those rules don't apply, since this is a non-international armed conflict. Such a fine distinction will not impress those at or near sites where drone attacks are raining down. The reasoning is redacted, but Barron also dismisses concerns about the denial of US Constitutional rights to a US citizen, though at least he recognizes that these rights do apply outside the country. This provides yet another example of the muddle resulting from hybrid theory, that combines both the international-war and law-enforcement perspectives.

THE INNOVATIVE KILL LIST

Administration critics such as Marjorie Cohn and Jeanne Mirer have noted that the fact that President Obama approves names for the kill list does not make it right or legal. Most victims of drone strikes are not US citizens, and most are not clearly militants, though, as Cohn and Mirer say, the Obama administration claims that it kills few civilians. This is primarily through re-definition because, under their doctrine of "signature strikes," they define military-age men killed in drone strikes as suspected combatants or militants. These signature strikes, unlike personality strikes, target groups exhibiting "suspicious patterns of behavior" rather than known individuals who are supposedly leaders or responsible militants. [8]

The idea of the kill list, in which the president actively manages the targeting of individuals on a weekly basis, is an innovation in US military policy. The process was developed early in the Obama era, but information wasn't revealed until 2012 and 2013 [9] thanks to the work of Glenn Greenwald and his colleagues at *The Intercept*. A whistle-blower also made *The Drone Papers* available, from which eight articles, a glossary, and original documents have been made public. They reveal that there is an interagency process involving lawyers and military advisors from the departments of State and Defense, the National Security Council, and the White House. These individuals meet via electronic conferencing and, having reviewed intelligence files, discuss and ultimately recommend to the President the appropriateness of drone surveillance and use of military force on individuals. On "Terror Tuesday" the President peruses names to add to the list, and sometimes he and his advisors will watch the attacks on what has been dubbed "Kill TV." [10] It is understood that this process only applies to those being monitored by the Department of Defense (DoD) in Yemen and Somalia and possibly others, and not those tracked by the CIA.

President Obama makes decisions on who goes on the list, but it is not clear whether this applies to even a majority of those who could be killed by the United States. The CIA directs the largest drone strike program—in Pakistan—and it is said that the President approves only one-third, at most, of attacks there. The level of casualties, those targeted as well as civilians, is unknown to the public. The Obama administration has consistently opposed disclosure of data on the number of targets and civilians killed, with considerable congressional support for its position. [11]

In *The Drone Papers*, Jeremy Scahill and his colleagues fill in the gaps in our knowledge of the drone warfare program. [12] The documents and interviews with the whistle-blower provide an account that differs greatly than that released for public consumption. The technological quick fix that is the drone program has a clear result—the desire and ability to kill rather than capture. The United States has neglected "human intelligence" (humint) and relies much more on "signal intelligence" (sigint). The country doesn't cultivate as many human sources, relying on high-tech information-gathering to complete the "baseball cards" on each target (a term that itself suggests the banality of the exercise). This means that a US drone strike may be on a cell phone rather than on the person who owns the phone or is thought to possess it. There is confirmation that drone strikes kill many people beyond the targeted terrorists, such as Operation Haymaker in 2011–2012 in the Hindu Kush area on the Afghan-Pakistan border. The "Enemy Killed in Action" classification is overused, allowing the claim that those killed are militants unless there is evidence otherwise. There is discussion about the gaps in drone surveillance because of the "tyranny of distance," the significant distance of drone bases from the area to be monitored, especially in Somalia and Yemen. This means even less certainty regarding who is actually being targeted as there is often not uninterrupted surveillance.

As an illustration of the kill-rather-than-capture incentive, consider the case of Bilal el-Berjawi, dubbed "objective Peckham," a British citizen who traveled back and forth from the United Kingdom and the Middle East. He was stripped of his citizenship and then killed in Somalia in a drone strike instead of being arrested in the United Kingdom.[13] These revelations confirm what critics have been saying for years, but so far they have had little impact on public opinion, in part because of the lack of North American media coverage. As a 2016 article by Kathy Gilsinan indicates, US drone use policy remains fluid. In May 2016 the United States broke new ground in announcing the death of Taliban leader Mullah Akhtar Muhammad Mansour. He was killed by a US drone strike in Quetta, Baluchistan, Pakistan, which happens to be the city that hosts the Taliban headquarters. Further, this was carried out by the US DoD and even tweeted to the public. That this was not a "covert" CIA operation but rather undertaken by DoD was an innovation, considering Pakistan is supposedly an ally in the war on terror.[14]

Even in the midst of general support for drone warfare, there are divisions among US senators regarding the appropriate home for control of the drone fleet. Republican senator John McCain has for many years advocated moving drone operations to the DoD because they are too numerous to simply be a branch within the CIA. Without saying so explicitly, he would be aware that the US government is vulnerable to war-crime charges because CIA officers not in military uniform are directing acts of war in violation of the Geneva Conventions. However, members of the Senate Intelligence Committee, including Democrat Diane Feinstein, former chair and now ranking minority member, oppose the move as does the Obama administration.[15] To some degree this is about bureaucratic turf, because keeping it in the CIA means it remains under the oversight purview of the Intelligence Committee. If moved, the drone program is vulnerable to critique at the hands of the Armed Service Committees of the House of Representatives and Senate. These committees are larger bodies with a more diverse membership, including liberal Democrats and libertarian Republicans who are less likely to share the national security consensus. The DoD is a line department that is more easily subject to congressional oversight, and less shielded by claims of national security and the need for secrecy compared to the CIA. The CIA's main focus is in Pakistan. It would be harder to operate through the DoD given the Pakistani government's stated opposition to the attacks and given the department's ongoing relationship with the Pakistani military. The drone program has natural enemies in Defense, whereas it faces no predators within the CIA.

Those who wanted to see a shift in US policy from CIA control of drones to Pentagon control got their way in July 2016 when the Obama administration issued a new executive order to move most drone activity to Defense. As the *Washington Post*'s Greg Miller wrote, there are a whole variety of background reasons for the policy shift. CIA drone strikes had declined in Pakistan in 2016. The Yemeni government that banned operations by Joint Special Operations Command collapsed, opening the door again to conventional military operations. The United States was also ready to turn Syria over to the Pentagon. Drone operations became so well known, whether directed by the CIA or DoD, that the CIA lost its secrecy advantage.[16] In other words, the United States would use the DoD openly in additional countries, including Syria, Yemen, and Pakistan, in addition to Afghanistan and Iraq. For his part, Robert Chesney comments that even after this shift the United States will still have a hybrid system between the CIA and DoD, based on a division of labor between the two agencies.[17]

QUESTION OF CONSTITUTIONALITY OF THE NEW WARFARE

The US courts, including the Supreme Court, have a history of being deferential to the executive branch in foreign- and military-policy matters. However, given the rise of new and unconventional warfare over the last fifteen years, the courts have taken greater interest in this realm. Some of the decisions that have come down from the US Supreme Court have potential to set a precedent that may eventually be used to restrict what the president can do when it comes to assassination, particularly via drones. The most suggestive decision since the beginning of the global war on terrorism is *Hamdi v. Rumsfeld*, which the Supreme Court issued in 2004.[18] This case is about an American citizen, Yaser Esam Hamdi, who was in Afghanistan on and after 9/11. He was seized by the local US ally, the Northern Alliance, and turned over to the US military on the grounds that he was captured with a weapon as part of a Taliban military unit. The plaintiff and his family contend that he was in Afghanistan briefly in the summer of 2001 to do aid work, and did not take military training or join a Taliban military unit. Hamdi was treated as an "enemy combatant," the new alternative to POW status. He was first moved to Guantanamo Bay. The military, upon learning that he was a US citizen, moved him to Navy brigs in Norfolk, Virginia, and then Charleston, South Carolina. The plaintiff and his family requested that the Supreme Court reverse the Fourth Circuit Court of Appeal and grant him a full judicial hearing to challenge his enemy-combatant status.

It came out that the designation of the plaintiff was based on the hearsay evidence of Michael Mobbs, identified as special advisor to the undersecretary of Defense for policy. Writing for the Court majority, Justice Sandra O'Connor concluded that: "We hold that although Congress authorized the detention of combatants in the narrow circumstances alleged here, due process demands that a citizen held in the United States as an enemy combatant be given a meaningful opportunity to contest the factual basis for that detention before a neutral decision maker."

How the Court came to this conclusion, as well as the concurrence from Justice David Souter, are both interesting but also suggestive of the means through which the Court might strike down the legitimacy of, or at least limit, drone warfare. The Court majority accepted that the AUMF of September 2011 was a legal declaration of war, and taking surrendered combatants as prisoners by the US military was acceptable during operations in Afghanistan. Interestingly, the Court majority affirms that the purpose of taking prisoners is "neither revenge, nor punishment," but rather it prevents a combatant from rejoining the fight. However, the Court recognizes the legitimacy of Hamdi's concern that this war may be indefinite, and therefore imprisonment may be too harsh. His concern is "not far-fetched" since even the US government concedes that "given its unconventional nature, the current conflict is unlikely to end with a formal cease-fire agreement." The Court also notes that the writ of habeas corpus has not been currently suspended, that citizens have the right to access the writ in the United States, where Hamdi now lives. The Court is aware that this case may create a "perverse incentive," in that in the future the US military may not bring the captured back to the United States, though the Court does not indicate any concern that "kill" may be substituted for "capture," as has in fact happened.

What comes next is perhaps most important from the perspective of the application of this case to drone warfare. The Court majority notes that the US government's position is that the judiciary should not interfere in the executive branch's prosecution of the global war on terrorism. However, if there is to be a judicial role, the executive branch argues that the courts should review the enemy combatant's status using only a minimal "some-evidence" standard. Instead of weighing the balance of evidence in favor and against, as we would normally see in a judicial process, the some-evidence standard means that "a court would assume the accuracy of the Government's articulated basis for Hamdi's detention, as set forth in the Mobbs

Declaration, and assess only whether the articulated basis was a legitimate one." The Court majority ultimately rejects as inadequate the government's position, saying that the detainee "must receive notice of the factual basis for his classification, and a fair opportunity to rebut the Government's factual assertions before a neutral decision maker."

The descriptions of the process for the Obama administration's drone program and kill list show that it only meets the some-evidence standard, rather than a more robust standard such as in *Hamdi*. The military and intelligence agencies build files and propose names of individuals to be killed by drone strike or other means, and the targeted person is not given an opportunity to "rebut the Government's factual assertions before a neutral decision maker." There is no advocate for the accused, not even one uninstructed by the accused. Even if the counter case is addressed in the kill-list process, there is no reason to think that those deliberating, including the president, would do anything beyond taking the military information at face value. And yet this process has been explicitly rejected by the Court, at least when it comes to an American citizen in custody in the United States. Of course, some will argue that the Court decision applies only to them. But is it so much of a stretch that these ideas would be applied to drone attacks overseas? Given the unconventional nature of the war, given weaknesses or human and surveillance intelligence, why shouldn't the Court eventually insist on a higher standard for executive branch assassination, especially if the war becomes permanent?

It is also worth mentioning that members of the Court, such as Justices Thomas, Scalia, and Stevens took a more conservative position than the majority, and dissented. Others such as Souter and Ginsburg concurred in the essentials but took a more liberal position. Justice Souter, writing for himself and Ginsburg, makes three points that could also pave the way for a rethinking of drone attacks and the kill list, should their views become more widely accepted on the Court. First, they don't accept that the AUMF actually authorizes the United States to take prisoners. They argue that such authorization needs to be more specific and explicit. One might say that this view could lead the same Justices to challenge whether the broad reading of the AUMF is correct, to the effect that it only authorizes US war in Afghanistan and not forever. Such a finding would present a challenge to the very heart of the expansion of the global war on terrorism.

Second, Souter points out that the government concedes that "the Geneva Convention applies to the Taliban detainees" and that, therefore, Hamdi "would seem to quality for treatment as a prisoner of war under the Third Geneva Convention." This means that the US government has violated the Convention in a number of ways, including holding Hamdi incommunicado for a long period. The Convention and the US Army regulation also have a robust process for a POW to challenge his status. Third, Souter points out that even the USA Patriot Act authorizes "the detention of alien terrorists for no more than seven days in the absence of criminal charges or deportation proceedings." He goes on to write: "It is very difficult to believe that the same Congress that carefully circumscribed Executive power over alien terrorists on home soil would not have meant to require the Government to justify clearly its detention of an American citizen held on home soil incommunicado." The current US drone program and kill list can only continue if there is acceptance that the country is at war on a global basis despite the lack of formal declarations. What if the Court decided that the United States couldn't expand its efforts in Yemen and other countries? In the current political climate would Congress dare to declare war on new fronts? A more aggressive Court could also deliver a blow to the new rules about indefinite detention that the United States is trying to put into place.

DEADLY FALLOUT FROM US POLICY

Few advocates of airborne assassination address the almost inevitable collateral damage, or the tendency of murder of the innocent to alienate and radicalize entire societies. Richard Belfield notes that assassination is very disruptive of domestic political systems, and one assassination either has followed others or leads to others.[19] In other words, assassination seems to be contagious. The Roman emperor Commodus, who succeeded Marcus Aurelius in 180 CE, was assassinated, leading to one hundred years in which political murder was the chief mechanism of imperial succession. The 1960s was the decade of assassination in the United States. While John F. Kennedy did not pull the trigger, he actively conspired to depose or assassinate Patrice Lumumba of the Congo, Ngo Dinh Diem of Vietnam, and Cuba's Fidel Castro. Kennedy himself fell in November 1963, a week after Diem in Vietnam, to be followed by Malcolm X, Martin Luther King, Jr., and Senator Robert Kennedy, as well as numerous lesser-known social activists, particularly African Americans. Assassination attempts have been made on virtually every president and many candidates since, and bullets found their targets, albeit nonfatally, in the cases of Governor George Wallace and President Ronald Reagan.

Writing before the large-scale effort to practice and legitimize assassination, Robert L. Holmes made the following comment: "Moral considerations aside, if one's quarrel is with the leadership of a country, and one believes in the use of violence, the more rational course [than conventional war] would be to engage in selective assassinations."[20] This would make leaders more accountable for their policies and might make them more cautious.

Secretary of Defense Donald Rumsfeld said that US forces would be welcomed as liberators in Iraq, though it is not clear whether he actually believed it. He and his successors *actually think* their dispute is only with leaders, so "take out" the leader (whether Saddam Hussein, bin Laden or Qaddafi) and problem solved. This is based in part on the power-politics tradition that says that foreign and defense policy is made exclusively by leaders. They lead according to their desire to preserve and increase their country's (and their own) power and treasure; the average citizen or subject has little to do with it. This theory never really came to terms with the change wrought by Napoleon Bonaparte and the Enlightenment era, in which people's willingness to support the state and to fight in war, or struggles for national liberation, is crucial. The reality is that to attack the country and kill the leader, who is often not as domestically unpopular as the "monster" created in the Western media for Western consumption, will increase the number of your opponents tenfold.

Trevor McCrisken cites Ikram Sehgal, of Pathfinder G4S, "Pakistan's largest private security firm," who estimates that seven to fifteen thousand "extremist students" attend pro-Taliban religious schools in any given year, and are among the sea of recruits for anti-Western militancy.[21] Once again the United States has created large numbers of opponents with emotional, rational, and spiritual reasons for their willingness to fight and die. Killing leaders does not deter people from taking their places. It is hard to see how military action, by either drone or conventional means, can achieve the Western world's stated political goals.

It would appear that there are as many or more experts with government experience who are concerned about the negative effects of drone warfare than there are those who accept the Bush-Obama line. Fred Branfman collected a list of those who have made statements, mostly after they retired, including: Adm. Dennis Blair, former director of National Intelligence; Michael Boyle, former Obama Counterterrorism advisor; Gen. James Cartwright, former vice-chair, Joint Chiefs of Staff; Micah Zenko, Council on Foreign Relations; Sherard Cowper-Coles, former UK special representative to Afghanistan; Mohammad Daudzai, former Afghan chief of staff; Robert Grenier, former head of the CIA Counterterrorism Center; Michael Hayden, former CIA director; Col. David Kilcullen, former David Petraeus Counterinsurgency advisor; Emile Nakhleh, senior CIA analyst; Gen. Stanley McChrystal; Cameron Munter, former US ambassador to Pakistan; Anne Patterson, ex-US ambassador to Pakistan; Bruce Riedel, Obama AfPak advisor; and Michael Scheueur, former CIA Counterterrorism operative.[22]

At one time, not so long ago, it was offensive to accuse the United States of being an "imperialist" state. Michael Parenti has written that in 1995 he was criticized for his title selection for one of his books on US foreign policy (*Against Empire*).[23] Such labeling was seen as an accusation hurled by the Soviet Union and its allies, by newly independent states in the Third World, and by the left-wing fringe in Europe or North America (or occasionally, by traditional conservatives like the Canadian George Grant or the Frenchman Raymond Aron).[24] More recently one can add political commentator Charles Krauthammer; the former leader of the Canadian Liberal Party, Michael Ignatieff; Anglo-Irish historian Niall Ferguson; and an increasing number of other mainstream academics and commentators. Perhaps it has become so obvious that few can deny it. The intellectual followers of Hans Morganthau and E. H. Carr, "the realists," have always quietly accepted the legitimacy, nay the necessity, of empire.

Even though such ideas were never meant for widespread public consumption, their advocates are now more open. As Parenti has written, "much of the historical literature on empire is rather favourable."[25] It could be added that there has often been an acceptance of imperial policies within the dominant state in real time, let alone in retrospect. It is fair to say that every empire in human history has claimed for itself noble motivations and a positive legacy. The reality is rather different, however, particularly for those wearing the yoke. At the core of any empire, however mild or "lite," to use Ignatieff's phrase, is the undue influence, or outright domination, of one state over another state or people. It seems that this domination, such as the United States over Afghanistan, Iraq, Bahrain, Pakistan, or Yemen, in whatever form it may take, cannot be sustained for long without popular uprising and either domestic or international enforcement of the power of the servile internal regime. The imperial power's tactics often become nasty because this is the only way to maintain the imperial state's position.

Under the Bush and Obama administrations, US tactics such as torture, summary execution, and assassination may be the subject of significant internal debate, but the history of empire shows that these are the tactics that a state *must* pursue in order to maintain its influence. A fascinating illustration of this was published in France in 2001, with an English translation in 2002. Retired French general Paul Aussaresses describes unapologetically and in great detail his pursuit of these tactics—torture, summary execution, and assassination—in Algeria from 1955–1957, particularly in Philippeville and Algiers.[26] In 1954, France had felt the blow of its defeat at its Vietnamese fortress at Dien Bien Phu; Algeria would be the French empire's last stand. Aussaresses describes his dispatch to Algeria and the ruthless tactics that he, other members of the French regular army, and local supporters pursued in trying to destroy the Algerian resistance, particularly the *Front de Libération Nationale*. The book confirms much of the content of the classic movie on the topic, *The Battle of Algiers* (1966, dir. Gillo Pantecorvo). Aussaresses describes the cases in which he oversaw or ordered torture, summary execution, and assassination, calling them what they were. He heartily defended his actions on the grounds that they were both known informally by his superiors (e.g., the responsible minister, and later president François Mitterrand), and was the only way to maintain Algeria's membership in the dwindling French empire. Aussaresses admits to having overseen the killing of 135 Algerians in one incident, adding that he had the decency to bury them in the Moslem cemetery "in a way that the bodies could lie in the direction of Mecca."[27] Bodies of dead Moslems are not always so sensitively handled by imperial powers.

CONCLUSION

Former US president Richard Nixon once said, "Well, when the president does it, that means it is not illegal." The arrogance and assumption behind that thinking might well be applied to the George W. Bush and Obama administrations as use of drone attacks and numbers of assassinations increase. They believe what they are doing is not only legal, but just. This chapter's argument, however, is that rather than performing actions that lead to peace in the world, US governments have managed to antagonize much of the Middle East and North Africa. The constitutionality of these actions is questionable, especially the infamous kill list. Together with the administration's drone program, it shows that it only meets the some-evidence standard rather than a more robust standard such as in the Supreme Court case of *Hamdi v. Rumsfeld*. It is vital to democracy to examine what a government feels it must do to maintain power and control inside and outside its own borders. While the administration may believe it has support for the drone program, there is some opposition, or at least questioning, even within the government and the CIA.

NOTES

1. G. William Domhoff, *Who Rules America?? The Triumph of the Corporate Rich*, 7th ed. (New York: McGraw Hill Education, 2014), 151.
2. Trevor McCrisken, "Ten years on: Obama's war on terrorism in rhetoric and practice," *International Affairs* 87(4 [2011]): 781–801.
3. Peter Bergen, "Drone Wars The Constitutional and Counterterrorism Implications of Targeted Killing," *New America*, April 24, 2014, https://www.newamerica.org/international-security/testimony-drone-wars/.
4. John Brennan, "The Ethics and Efficacy of the President's Counterterrorism Strategy," Woodrow Wilson Center for Scholars, Washington, DC, April 30, 2012.
5. Michael S. Paulsen, "Drone On: The Commander in Chief Power to Target and Kill Americans," *Harvard Journal of Law and Public Policy* 38(1 [2014]): 61.
6. Ibid., 43–61.
7. David Barron, "Memorandum for the Attorney General," Department of Justice, Office of Legal Counsel, July 16, 2010, http://cdn1.vox-cdn.com/assets/4656273/dronememo.pdf.
8. Marjorie Cohn and J. Mirer, "Killer Drone Attacks Illegal, Counter-Productive," *Huffington Post*, June 25, 2012, www.huffingtonpost.com, June 25, 2012.
9. McCrisken, "Obama's Drone War," *Survival: Global Politics and Strategy* 55(2 [2013]): 97–122.
10. Daniel Klaidman, "Drones: The Silent Killers." *Newsweek*, May 28, 2012, http://www.newsweek.com/drones-silent-killers-64909.

11. Spencer Ackerman, "US senators remove requirement for disclosure over drone strike victims," *The Guardian*, April 28, 2014, http://www.theguardian.com/world/2014/apr/28/drone-civilian-casualties-senate-bill-feinstein-clapper.

12. The documents are available at https://theintercept.com/drone-papers/.

13. A good summary of the project is found in J. Scahill, "The Assassination Complex," October 15, 2015, https://theintercept.com/drone-papers/.

14. Kathy Gilsinan, "The Drone War Crosses Another Line," *The Atlantic*, May 23, 2016, http://www.theatlantic.com/international/archive/2016/05/drone-mullah-akhtar-taliban/483863/.

15. Ackerman, see note 11 above.

16. Greg Miller, "Why CIA drone strikes have plummeted," *Washington Post*, June 16, 2016, https://www.washingtonpost.com/world/national-security/cia-drone-strikes-plummet-as-white-house-shifts-authority-to-pentagon/2016/06/16/e0b28e90-335f-11e6-8ff7-7b6c1998b7a0_story.html.

17. Robert Chesney, "Shift to JSOC on Drone Strikes Does Not Mean CIA Has Been Sidelined," Lawfare, June 16, 2016, https://www.lawfareblog.com/shift-jsoc-drone-strikes-does-not-mean-cia-has-been-sidelined.

18. The *Hamdi v. Rumsfeld* decision (June 28, 2004) concurrences and dissents are found at https://supreme.justia.com/cases/federal/us/542/507/#annotation.

19. Richard Belfield, *The Assassination Business: A History of State-Sponsored Murder*, New York: Carroll & Graf, 2005.

20. Robert Holmes, *On War and Morality* (Princeton, NJ: Princeton University Press, 1989), 262.

21. McCrisken, see note 9 above.

22. Fred Branfman, "Even the Warriors Say the Wars Make Us Less Safe," WorldBeyond-War.org, http://worldbeyondwar.org/lesssafe/.

23. Michael Parenti, *The Face of Imperialism* (Boulder and London: Paradigm Publishers, 2011), 5.

24. George Grant, *Lament for a Nation: The Defeat of Canadian Nationalism*, 1965, Montreal-Kingston: McGill-Queen's UP, 2005; Raymond Aron, *The Imperial Republic*, Englewood Cliffs, NJ: Prentice Hall, 1974.

25. Parenti, see note 22 above.

26. Paul Aussaresses, *The Battle of the Casbah: Terrorism and Counter-Terrorism in Algeria, 1955–1957* (New York: Enigma Books, 2002).

27. Ibid., 51–52.

Chapter Three

Military, Markets, and Money

To truly understand the new way of war and the normalization of permanent war, one needs to look seriously at the US military industry. This necessitates recounting scandals about the provision of military materiel as far back as the US Civil War and World War I. But it is also inevitably a discussion about the rise and dominance of the military-industrial complex (MIC) in US society. This involves the collective interests of thousands of military suppliers, as well as states and congressional districts with military bases and manufacturing plants. Part of the sordid tale are elected politicians who stand to gain from reelection when they make decisions based only on their perception of their own state's economic interest, not to mention postretirement return of favors from military contractors. All this isn't new. Although the term MIC was not coined until the late 1950s, the concept was evident in American politics long before that.

As this chapter will show, sometimes this issue is also about a single major player, such as Lockheed Martin, which can easily stand in for all the vices of a sector. From this perspective, the rise of drone warfare is just a new frontier for the MIC. These multinational corporations and subsidiaries will have an interest in the cultivation of global markets for any military product, even if that runs against the interest of the United States and its NATO allies. The MIC also has privileged access to public resources and since 9/11 can spend in ways that are unknown in the rest of the public sector. Connections between industry, government, and the military are tight, and in many cases they are questionable. While government representatives are focused on keeping their home states happy, who is looking at the bigger picture, ensuring that decisions are made in a just and equitable way? In the early 1980s there was a quip to the effect that the "United States has a

Military-Industrial Complex but the Soviet Union is one." It now looks like the United States is one as well.

THE ROLE OF THE MILITARY-INDUSTRIAL COMPLEX

The classic view of the US government is that Congress, assumed to be a good reflection of the opinions of American voters, creates a budget and makes policies and laws that the presidency then executes. If the voters are unhappy with the performance of the legislative or executive branches, then they can vote for different candidates who promise and execute change. This may never have been an accurate rendering of the political process, and it is now a quaint vision that doesn't remotely capture how government works and how change does and (mostly) does not happen. An alternative idea is that the United States has a "permanent government," with external social and internal bureaucratic forces that exercise significant influence regardless of the competition between Democrats and Republicans. Acceptance of this idea goes well beyond those who wear tinfoil hats—believers in conspiracy theories. One such form of this permanent government is the MIC. James Ledbetter describes it as "a network of public and private forces that combine a profit motive with the planning and implementation of strategic policy."[1]

President Dwight D. Eisenhower cited MIC in his farewell address as President in 1961. This is an excerpt:

> Now this conjunction of an immense military establishment and a large arms industry is new in the American experience. The total influence—economic, political, even spiritual—is felt in every city, every statehouse, every office of the federal government. We recognize the imperative need for this development. Yet we must not fail to comprehend its grave implications. Our toil, resources, and livelihood are all involved. So is the very structure of our society.
>
> In the councils of government, we must guard against the acquisition of unwarranted influence, whether sought or unsought, by the military-industrial complex. The potential for the disastrous rise of misplaced power exists and will persist. We must never let the weight of this combination endanger our liberties or democratic processes.

While the idea behind the MIC was not new in 1961—Ledbetter points out that the radical sociologist C. Wright Mills published the basic idea a few years earlier in his now-classic book *The Power Elite*[2] —this was the first time the general public heard the terminology. Eisenhower was no radical, but he was something of an American traditionalist. He knew the reality of the military and of war, as a career military man and Supreme Allied Commander in Europe in World War II. He did not take war lightly, unlike some of his successors. Part of Eisenhower's traditionalism took the form of a belief in limited, republican, competent government. Most importantly he would not pander to what he regarded as uninformed public opinion or the opportunism of the unscrupulous. Part of these traditional values included the idea that elected people, rather than civil servants and military officers, would actually make key decisions and be accountable for them. As Ledbetter reminds us, Eisenhower spent much of his eight years in office resisting calls from Democrats and more conservative Republicans for more military interventions and increased spending on effective—and ineffective—weapons systems. He had no patience for interservice rivalries in the military or other such inefficiencies.

For example, the United States might have introduced combat troops into Vietnam in 1956 had Eisenhower not given a firm "no" when some of his advisors urged it.[3] His advocacy of nuclear disarmament was at odds with a majority of the country and the Democratic Party. The Democrats used the Soviet Union's launch of the first satellite (Sputnik) into orbit to score political points and to advocate for more military spending than Eisenhower thought was acceptable or prudent. They also criticized him for cancelling the B-70 bomber, which was to replace the B-52. He decried weapons manufacturers like Boeing that were taking out full-page advertisements to sway opinion toward purchasing their products (such as the Bomarc missile system) regardless of performance. Perhaps the greatest injustice was the alleged "missile gap" of 1960, which John F. Kennedy used to good effect to be elected president over Eisenhower's sitting vice president. It was based, in part, on the false claim that the Soviet Union had a missile advantage.[4]

While the MIC concept highlighted a situation that was visible by the late 1950s, it had been around for several generations, whenever there were opportunities for war profiteering. As Ledbetter notes, other theses had been proposed: the *merchant of death* thesis that arms dealers cause and exacerbate wars for their own self-interest; the *war economy* thesis that so much of the economy is tied into military production that a dangerous interdependence between government and arms manufacturers is created; the *garrison state* thesis that because of twentieth-century global wars and the Cold War, the world has become more militarized in its social organization, at the expense of civil liberties and democratic ideas; and the *technocratic elite* thesis that in an increasingly complex technological society, unaccountable bureaucrats wield the real power in place of elected governments.[5]

According to Ledbetter, there are numerous cases in the nineteenth and early twentieth centuries that supported these theories. During the US Civil War, concerns were widespread about the provision of substandard materiel at inflated prices. In the 1890s, the "iron plate trust" was identified in which steel companies, particularly Carnegie Steel, sold substandard iron plate to the US military and colluded to prevent exposure. As the result of an 1894 investigation, a division of Carnegie Steel paid a fine of $140,000 for this and for deceiving government inspectors about product certification.

During World War I, Rep. C. H. Tavenner called for nationalization of the armaments industry to take away the private, for-profit, pro-war pressures. In the 1930s, North Dakota senator Gerald Nye launched an investigation, known as the Munitions Inquiry, which followed up on arms dealings and also flirted with the idea that the United States should be officially and legally neutral in other countries' conflicts. Nye's initiatives stepped on the toes of the growing arms industry, and many in the Roosevelt administration, but he was ultimately discredited by introducing documents challenging the idea of former president Woodrow Wilson as the idealist who was unaware of and opposed to European power politics during the war.[6]

The 1980s is referred to as the Reagan era, but there was also a strong current of primarily Democratic dissent against the scaling up of militarism. Ronald Dellums, representative from Berkeley, California, led the opposition to Reagan's pursuit of what international relations scholar Fred Halliday[7] called the "second cold war" against the Soviet Union. Picking up from the realist turn late in the Carter administration, the Reaganites were aggressively anti-Soviet and also pursued a nuclear-war–fighting doctrine with its new generation of weapons systems. Dellums' response was to organize special congressional hearings against the Reagan proposals, with testimony from leading experts in political, economic, and moral elements of rising militarism and a revived nuclear arms race. He developed an alternative US military budget slashing $50 billion from the 1983 budget (proposed by Reagan to be $258 billion).[8] He envisioned a purely defensive military, with cuts to new weapons systems and troop deployments designed to extend US power globally. Remarkably, the House of Representatives Rules Committee allowed his bill to compete in July 1982 with the Armed Services Committee bill on the House floor, though of course the victory of the latter was never in doubt.[9]

EXHIBIT A: LOCKHEED MARTIN

As William D. Hartung points out in his 2012 book on Lockheed Martin,[10] one can trace the history of the MIC through the trajectory of this now-merged super-company. Lockheed Martin is rooted in the 1916 founding of Lougheed Aircraft Company. Every element of the MIC is found in its history: sale of arms to combatants, despite the Neutrality Act and without federal response; government bailouts to avoid bankruptcy; weapon system underperformance that is met with governmental denial; scandals centered on cost overruns and the high cost of additional weapons and spare parts; and government promotion of the arms industry as a sunrise export business.

Despite US government neutrality in the late 1930s, producers like Lockheed sold weapons to all sides. This included the Electra, the civilian transport plane that was easily converted to military purposes and was the basis for the Hudson bomber during World War II. In September 1939, Congress made it illegal for US citizens to provide war materiel to the belligerents in Europe. Lockheed's response was to fly Hudson bombers to an airfield straddling the Canadian border and then push the planes across to be transported to the United Kingdom. Canada was at war with Germany at the time but was not an active combatant until months later.[11]

Many of the vices of the MIC are tangled up together, including the role of influential legislators, the green-lighting of substandard military designs, the availability of money, the role of whistle-blowers and the price they pay, government bailouts to preserve the "defense industrial base," and the revolving door between the DoD and military contractors. One of the best cases is Lockheed Martin's C-5A Galaxy, the world's largest military transport plane. During the 1960s, the US military decided to commission a new, larger transport plane to replace the C-130 Hercules: it would be 260-feet long, with a 230-feet wingspan, a tail seven stories tall, and would be required to land on dirt runways only four thousand feet in length. The main competition came down to Lockheed and Boeing. The USAF's choice was Boeing, but then the pork barrel and Lockheed's superior lobbying effort went into high gear. Lockheed told Rep. Mandel Rivers of Charleston, South Carolina, that it would relocate jobs to his city if he ensured that their design was built. Rivers had as his campaign slogan "Rivers Delivers," and as chair of the House Armed Services Committee he could make sure he did, particularly in that long-past era of a stronger role for congressional committee chairs. Add to that the support of Georgia senator Richard Russell (for whom one of the Senate office buildings is now named), who was chair of the Senate Armed Services Committee, a powerful force on the Appropriations Committee, and a confidante of President Lyndon Johnson. He wanted the jobs for Marietta, Georgia, and he would have his way.[12]

This was the first use of a new procurement system with all its unintended consequences, a brainchild of Defense secretary Robert S. McNamara. Total package procurement (TPP) was like "design-build" in the construction industry, when all aspects of the job are handled by the same firm, from architecture through landscaping, producing a turnkey result. In TPP, however, the bidders would need to estimate costs ten, fifteen, or twenty years out from concept to the end of production. In addition, a company could not do research and development (R and D) on a weapons system unless it was guaranteed to go into production. The government could not afford to or would not fund multiple contractors to do full designs for competing products. With the R and D contract, the company would also get the production contract. This would make it even easier for arms producers to practice *buy-*

in or *bait-and-switch*, in which the company underestimates total costs knowing that it will have the government over a barrel later and can reap major returns. Lockheed kept coming back for more money for the C-5A, while also increasing the price for phase II purchases, knowing that the government would not cancel the program with only half a fleet.[13]

We would know far less about quality problems and cost overruns of the C-5A were it not for the public disclosures of Ernie Fitzgerald, a civilian cost estimator employed by the USAF. While the congressional armed-services committees were prepared to sweep rumors under the carpet, two Pennsylvanians, the legendary senator William Proxmire and Rep. William Moorehead, used their congressional committees to call Fitzgerald and other witnesses. After his testimony, Fitzgerald was transferred to new DoD duties assessing costs of food services and bowling alley construction. He did, however, still receive documents from colleagues that he was able to pass on. The Air Force Office of Special Investigations failed to find dirt on him but then claimed that he had distributed secret information. Even though Fitzgerald was granted career tenure under civil service rules, in November 1969 he was fired, based on the claim that he was given job security through a computer error. Though eventually rehired, it would be years before he could do meaningful work. As Hartung points out, the documentary record shows that President Nixon approved his dismissal.[14]

By 1969 and into the early 1970s, the battle had shifted to addressing the C-5A's deficiencies and the question of whether the USAF would buy a second run. A Lockheed supervisor named Henry Dunham emerged to tell of waste and management at the Marietta, Georgia, factory and of overpricing spare parts at taxpayers' expense. In order to save Lockheed, which was at risk of bankruptcy, the USAF decided to purchase a second batch of planes, beyond the fifty-three in the first order. The contract allowed Lockheed to recoup $670 million in losses in the first run (this was after the USAF contributed $500 million to those overruns), by increasing the price of the planes in the second run. On the eve of congressional hearings with only four planes delivered, the decision was taken to put in the order. As Hartung says, concerns about the plane's performance did not require special study, as there were public incidents with cracked wings, engines falling off, and blown tires. As well, the plane did not meet expected landing standards.[15] Despite all this, Congress backed up the USAF in buying additional planes, paying for overruns, and creating a $200-million "slush fund" to keep Lockheed going. The company was also in trouble because of problems with its civilian airliner, the L-1011 Tristar.[16] But, as is so often the case, even liberal Democrats, like Senator Alan Cranston of California, voted for the bill to save jobs in their home states and districts.

Another example of conflict of interest, incompetence, and lack of accountability is found in the Cheyenne program. In 1967, the US government was looking for a replacement for the Cobra helicopter, and Lockheed had an idea—build an aircraft that takes off like a helicopter but flies like a fixed-wing aircraft. The company received developmental funds for two years, even though it had never built a helicopter, let alone a complicated design that was to perform more like a British-style "jump jet" than a Cobra or a Hughie. In that time Cheyenne experienced a cost-estimate increase from $1 million to $3 million, as well as a series of design and performance deficiencies. In March 1969 a prototype crashed, killing the pilot. One month later the US Army laid down an ultimatum that the problems must be fixed or the project would be cancelled.

Despite sinking $500 million into the project, only ten prototypes were produced, instead of the planned run of 375 aircraft. It turned out that one of the chief advocates of the Cheyenne, Willis Hawkins, was a former Lockheed executive hired by the Army in the mid-1960s. According to Hartung, Hawkins sold his Lockheed stock when he entered government service, though he still received deferred compensation. Hawkins and his assistant, Gen. William W. Dick, Jr., were then hired by Lockheed as the Cheyenne program collapsed. This was only the tip of the iceberg; Senator Proxmire issued a report stating that in 1969, two thousand former civilian and military federal employees went to work for major defense contractors, including 210 for Lockheed.[17]

As well as supporting other programs, including the L-1011, and funding cost overruns, two years later the House of Representatives voted 192–189 in favor of the Nixon administration's request for a loan guarantee of $250 million for Lockheed. Despite furious debate, the measure also passed by 49–48 in the Senate, advocated by former Texas governor John Connally and with the support of twenty-two Senate Democrats and opposed by seventeen free-market Republicans.[18]

SCANDAL AFTER SCANDAL

As time has passed, new signs of the role of Lockheed in the MIC have come to light. In the early 1980s the search was on for a new generation supercargo plane. The internal USAF process favored a McDonnell Douglas design, dubbed the C-17, over Lockheed's proposed C-5B. Some congressional forces, such as Washington's senator Henry "Scoop" Jackson, favored a transport version of the Boeing 747, which happened to be made in his home state. But a leaked ninety-six-page lobbying document from inside the Pentagon showed how integrated Lockheed was with the DoD. It laid out the plan to convince Congress to buy Lockheed's successor to the expensive and troubled C-5A Galaxy, including which prominent current and former officials would lobby which members of Congress. Lockheed would even write the Defense secretary's position paper on the C-5B, and the "Dear Colleague" letter that C-5B advocates in Congress would send to other members.

One tactic was to pitch to Congress the idea that this would create jobs, not only for the main contractor, but also the subcontractors. Because of the location of military and civilian manufacturing, this meant that a majority of both houses could be cobbled together in support of a new weapons system, no matter how wasteful.[19] As Hartung says, "[a] by-product of this process is that liberal members who often denounce waste and abuse in the military budget suddenly become ardent military budget boosters when it comes to the weapons built in their states and districts."[20] Similar stories can also be told about other Lockheed Martin systems, such as the F-22 and the F-35 Joint Strike Fighter.

It is sad to say that private contractors and their governmental overseers are not above faking test results. This was the case for Lockheed's Homing Overlay Experiment, which was central to Ronald Reagan's Strategic Defense Initiative (SDI), popularly called Star Wars. In what could be termed "operation stocked pond," a General Accounting Office report in the 1990s confirmed that a 1984 successful test was, in fact, faked. The target warhead was easier to hit than if it were in a combat situation because it sent out a signal to help the interceptor find its target, it was heated up for the heat-sensing equipment, and it was turned sideways to provide a bigger target. Hartung reports that the Pentagon considered but then abandoned the idea of explosives in the missile so that it could be detonated whether or not it was hit. All these plans were characterized as in the "national interest" because they were designed to intimidate the Soviet Union. They were very much in Lockheed's interest as well, since it meant the money would keep flowing.[21]

The C-5B may have seemed to be just another bailout of Lockheed, but the best was yet to come. Lockheed Martin was created in 1995 as a merger between Lockheed and Martin Marietta, but in part it was done with government money. John Deutsch and William Perry, Clinton defense officials with industry connections, recommended that there be a policy change at the Pentagon to allow the US government to fund "defense industry restructuring" such as "closing plants, relocating equipment, paying severance to laid-off workers, and providing 'golden parachutes' to board members and executives." The rationale for government support was that it would lead to savings on weapons systems, though that is hard to demonstrate given the complexity of those contractual relationships. As a result of an investigation by then-representative Bernie Sanders (I-VT), it was revealed that the new Lockheed Martin benefitted to the tune of $1.8 billion. This included payment from the Clinton administration for one-third of $92 million in severance for displaced executive and board members. Norman Augustine, former Martin Marietta CEO and new Lockheed Martin CEO, actually received $8.2 million in severance even though he received what amounted to a promotion in the process! Sanders succeeded in putting limits on this in the fiscal year 1996 budget. Augustine gave the government-funded portion of his package to charity, but most of the money Lockheed Martin received was untouched by lawmakers. There was also enough negative publicity to prevent either public funding or regulatory approval for a takeover of, or merger with, Northrup Grumman.[22]

NEW MARKETS FOR THE MIC

The end of the Cold War and the expansion of NATO have been a boom for companies like Lockheed Martin because new members have an incentive to replace their domestic or Soviet-era hardware with NATO-compatible, and especially US-compatible, weapons and equipment. Hartung reports that US arms exports increased from $11 billion in 2000 to $46 billion in 2011, some of it from sales to the Middle East, including Saudi Arabia and Iraq. While Lockheed Martin is not on the ground floor of the development of new drone technology, it is making sure it can take advantage of the increasing market for the aircraft. The company produces the Hellfire missile, which is now a standard part of drone weapons packages. It also makes the RQ-170 surveillance drone, the Desert Hawk III mid-drone, and the Stalker. Add to this an unmanned truck, the "ox," and being in the running to build a next-generation unmanned bomber.[23] In February 2015, the State Department announced that the United States will allow the export of weaponized drone technology, with safeguards,[24] to take advantage of a global market that is expected to double over the next ten years.

Even when the DoD and executive branch wants to cancel a system, Congress, so permeated by MIC interests, sometimes reverses the decisions. In 2012, for example, Defense decided to cancel the RQ-4 Global Hawk program, only to have it revived by Congress a year later after a robust lobbying campaign by drone maker Northrop Grumman. According to research by the Center for Responsive Politics, that year Grumman spent $17.5 million in lobbying, up from $11 million in 2011. And the company spent another $14 million in the first three-quarters of 2013.[25] In September 2015 Grumman was awarded a $3.2 billion contract to provide technical upgrades and spare parts for the Global Hawk fleet.[26] It was announced in early 2016 that five Golden Hawks would be sold and delivered to NATO by the end of that year, and based in Italy.[27] They are high-altitude surveillance planes slated to replace the aging U-2 spy planes, though there is no agreement on when.

The rise of Drone Nation can be associated with the products of General Atomics, such as the Predator. Not only are US firms actively cultivating global markets, but drone design and production have become truly global as well. As Christopher Harress has written, besides General Atomics there are at least eleven other global players poised to enter the market with drone products to transform the global military in ways that only science fiction authors once imagined. This list includes American companies Boeing, Lockheed Martin, Northrop Grumman, AeroVironment Inc., SAIC, Textron, and General Dynamics; Prox Dynamics AS from Norway; Denel Dynamics from South Africa; China's DJI; and last, but not least, Israel Aerospace Industries—one of the early pioneers of drone technology.[28] The competition for global markets is fierce and even those countries identified as possible future adversaries, such as Russia and China, are now important potential markets.[29]

A sign of the embeddedness of the MIC in US society is its ubiquity. In a recent edited collection called *MIC at 50* [years], David Swanson outlines the reality in Virginia, his home state. Virginia is one of the most militarized states in the union, but almost every state has a similar story. There are facilities there run by the National Ground Intelligence Center; the National Geo-Spatial Intelligence Agency; the Defense Intelligence Agency; the Judge Advocate General; the Virginia National Guard; the Pentagon; the CIA headquarters in Langley and Camp Peary, a.k.a. The Farm; the National Counter-Terrorism Intelligence Center; the FBI Academy at Quantico; the National Reconnaissance Office; Office of Naval Intelligence; and the Mount Weather Emergency Operations Center. Add to this dozens of USA, USAF, and USMC bases and facilities, and hundreds of private contractors.[30]

Even in a stagnant economy with a declining middle class, the MIC is affluent. The military doesn't take a pay cut, nor are its benefits under threat for active members. As former diplomat Peter Van Buren writes, "The military pays well; no scrambling for a minimum wage at Camp LeJeune. With combat pay more or less standard since 9/11 (the whole world being a battlefield, of course), the Congressional Budget Office estimates that the average active duty service member receives a benefits and pay compensation package worth $99,000." Service members receive a defined-benefit pension after twenty years or more of service, as well as free medical and dental care, subsidized housing, a clothing allowance, and more. The Pentagon is the world's largest operator of golf courses (234),[31] a standard feature at military bases. No signs of urban decay either: "Streets are well maintained, shaded by tall trees planted there (and regularly pruned) for just that purpose. Road, water, and sewer crews are always working. There are no potholes. There is a single school with a prominent football field, and a single shopping area." On-base retail does not charge sales tax and by law must be nonprofit.[32] Commenting on its excellent subsidized child care and higher education, Nicholas Kristof went so far as to call it "our lefty military."[33]

Both the global war on terrorism and the rise of Drone Nation have meant that the MIC is strengthened in another way. It has been known for some time that the United States employed "military contractors" on the ground in Afghanistan and Iraq, and that the intelligence establishment has made widespread use of private contractors to enable the expansion in signal intelligence gathering and analysis (Edward Snowden's job). What is also clear is that private contractors are very active in the drone program, particularly as analysts. Drawing from a Bureau of Investigative Journalism study, *The Guardian* reported in 2015 that one in ten intelligence analysts working on drone and spy-plane footage are nonmilitary civilian contractors. "Though private contractors do not formally make life-and-death choices—only military personnel operate armed drones and take final targeting decisions—there is concern that they could creep into this function without more robust oversight."[34] Let us add that it is an iron law of contemporary US (and probably Western) politics that privatization breeds more privatization, because unlike public bodies, private corporations make campaign contributions that become useful for legislators seeking reelection.

Ellen Brown, a well-known advocate for public banking and economic reform, sums it up well: "The MIC currently drags down the real economy in a variety of ways. The MIC and MIC-related activities account for over a trillion dollars of federal spending each year, and the military provides the closest thing the US has to an industrial policy and a jobs program. The political dynamics of the US are such that increased military spending is the only form of spending that 'gets a pass from the deficit hawks.'" The military provides much-needed funding to university researchers and diverts the best minds away from civilian innovation. She notes that production for the military has "built-in obsolescence," because war materiel is either blown up or has a limited shelf life. There has been a long-standing recognition that domestic spending on education, health care, transportation, green energy, and industrial investment provides a greater economic impact in the short term. In the longer term it generates economic growth through a better educated, healthier population with access to more efficient transportation, more sustainable energy, and a more productive and up-to-date economy. Because of the hold of the MIC, the country's major industrial export is military hardware. The US taxpayer is the first customer.[35] Because war is profitable, it results in permanent war.

CONCLUSION

This chapter has illustrated the power of the MIC as it neatly combines profit for corporate America with decision making by the US government. Despite early calls for nationalization of the armaments industry, it was allowed to grow, creating wealth for companies and opportunities for politicians. Industry lobbying has resulted in questionable decisions about planes, armaments, and other military materiel. The history of the MIC can actually be traced through the history of what became Lockheed Martin. The company's story is the story of the MIC—sale of arms to combatants, government bailouts to avoid bankruptcy, weapon systems' underperformance, cost scandals, and government promotion of the arms industry. While the company does not create new drone technology, it is taking advantage of the increasing market for drone aircraft. Competition in the global drone market is fierce. The industry will double before the next decade ends, and its influence will continue to be felt. Conflicts of interest, contradictions over what is really in the interests of the citizenry, and who deserves to profit, are all compelling issues to be considered.

NOTES

1. James Ledbetter, *Unwarranted Influence: Dwight D. Eisenhower and the Rise of the Military-Industrial Complex* (New Haven, CT and London: Yale University Press, 2011), 6.
2. Ibid., 15–16.
3. *Foreign Relations of the United States, 1952–1954*, vol. XIII: *Indochina* (Washington, DC: US Department of State, 1982), 1253.
4. Ledbetter, chap. 4. See note 1 above.
5. Ibid., 17–18.
6. Ibid., 19–26.
7. Fred Halliday, *The Making of the Second Cold War* (New York: Verso, 1987).
8. CQ Almanac, "Defense 1982: Overview."
9. Ronald V. Dellums, with R. H. Miller and H. L. Halterman, *Defense Sense: The Search for a Rational Military Policy* (Cambridge, MA: Ballinger Publishing Company, 1983), xix.
10. William D. Hartung, *Prophets of War: Lockheed Martin and the Making of the Military-Industrial Complex* (New York: Nation Books, 2012).
11. Ibid., 45–47.
12. Ibid., 70–72.
13. Ibid., 74–75.
14. Ibid., 78–81.
15. William D. Hartung, *Prophets of War: Lockheed Martin and the Making of the Military-Industrial Complex*, New York: Nation Books, 2012.
16. Ibid., 91–94.
17. Ibid., 100–103.
18. Ibid., 105–114.
19. Ibid., 150–52.
20. Ibid., 155.
21. Ibid., 159–61.
22. Ibid., 172–75.
23. Ibid., 265–67.
24. US Department of State, "U.S. Export Policy for Military Unmanned Aerial Systems," February 17, 2015, http://www.state.gov/r/pa/prs/ps/2015/02/237541.htm.
25. Brandon Conradis, "Northrop Grumman's Drone Campaign."
26. Andrea Shalal, "Northrop wins U.S. Global Hawk drone contract worth up to $3.2 billion," Reuters, September 30, 2015, http://www.reuters.com/article/us-northrop-grumman-globalhawk-idUSKCN0RU2UT20150930.
27. Anna Forrester, "Northrop Grumman to Deliver 5 Global Hawks to NATO," *Executive-Biz*, January 27, 2016, http://blog.executivebiz.com/2016/01/defense-news-nato-air-base-in-italy-to-take-in-5-northrop-global-hawks-by-years-end/.

28. Christopher Harress, "12 Companies That Will Conquer the Drone Market In 2014 and 2015," *International Business News*, January 10, 2014, http://www.ibtimes.com/12-companies-will-conquer-drone-market-2014–2015–1534360.

29. Daniel A. Medina, "Drone markets open in Russia, China and rogue states as America's wars wane," *The Guardian*, June 22, 2016, http://www.theguardian.com/business/2014/jun/22/drones-market-us-military-china-russia-rogue-state.

30. David Swanson, "Your Local Military Industrial Complex," in *The Military-Industrial Complex at 50* (Charlottesville, VA: 2011), 23–33.

31. "Military golf courses come under fire," www.PGA.com.

32. Peter Van Buren, "This Land Isn't Your Land, This Land Is Their Land," May 1, 2014, http://zcomm.org/znetarticle/this-land-isnt-your-land-this-land-is-their-land/.

33. Nicholas D. Kristof, "Our Lefty Military," *New York Times*, June 15, 2011, http://www.nytimes.com/2011/06/16/opinion/16kristof.html?_r=0.

34. Abigail Fielding-Smith et al., "Revealed: Private firms at heart of US drone warfare," *The Guardian*, July 30, 2015, http://www.theguardian.com/us-news/2015/jul/30/revealed-private-firms-at-heart-of-us-drone-warfare.

35. Ellen Brown, "The Military as a Jobs Program," in *Military-Industrial Complex*, 92–97. See note 17 above.

Chapter Four

Inside the Military Machine

As the Vietnam War dragged on with increasing numbers of young American men coming home in caskets, public support in the United States greatly declined. Years later the term "Vietnam syndrome" was coined as a description of America's aversion to involvement in any international war. Today Drone Nation can be seen as a response to that syndrome because the revolution in satellite communication, computerization, and the remote control of aircraft flight makes a "shadow war" possible. US forces can strike at adversaries without much domestic public awareness. [1]

As Jeremy Packer and J. Reeves comment, the concept of a world war has had many manifestations since the early twentieth century—World Wars I and II, and the Cold War. To this list they add the drone warfare era. For governments it is a commitment to the "global battlespace" war without human error. [2] And it is the latest in a long line of developments that seek to reinforce the idea that military air power is, relatively speaking, the closest thing to a "virtuous war." [3] Continual technological improvements have finally enabled the goal of centralizing control over air combat and increasing its "efficiency." This will be illustrated in this chapter by describing how drone warfare is organized within the US military.

Drone warfare has changed how the US military operates. Most importantly, the role of the pilot has greatly evolved. The image of the fit, skilled, uniformed fighter pilot has essentially gone out the window to be replaced by a pilot that is somewhat detached from the task. Ground crews have a greater role and decisions are made remotely. It's worth considering the differences between drone pilots and traditional cockpit pilots. And with these role changes come new problems of stress and culpability.

Most of what follows is about the drone experience in the USAF. Although the Central Intelligence Agency (CIA) is deeply involved in the drone business, it has not been as transparent in how its system works.

IT'S A BOY!

Drones in the US military and the CIA have gone from a small number of aircraft doing surveillance, to larger, more rugged aircraft carrying heavier weapons, allowing them to play an offensive role. Increasingly sophisticated drone aircraft has appeared over the last fifteen years, with promises of innovation to come. The USAF has made major commitments to three vehicles: the MQ-1B Predator, the MQ-9 Reaper, and the RQ-4 Global Hawk. Each has its purpose and each is equally menacing.

The Predator is referred to as a Medium-Altitude, Long-Endurance (MALE) aircraft, powered by a 115 horsepower gas engine with a top speed of 135 mph. It can fly as high as 25,000 feet, weighs only 1,130 pounds but can carry 450 pounds of payload. It can stay in the air forty hours, has a range of 454 miles, and, when armed, carries two laser-guided AGM-1154 Hellfire missiles. Also a MALE, the Reaper is bigger, heavier, faster, and with a longer range. It can spend fourteen hours in the air when fully armed. It carries eight times the payload of the Predator with a combination of Hellfire missiles, GBU-12 Paveway IIs, and GBU-38 Joint Direct Attack Munitions (JDAM).

The Paveway II is a laser-guided, 500-pound bomb, and the JDAM is an "add-on" guidance system that uses Global Positioning System (GPS) technology for the missile. The Predator and the Reaper are built by General Atomics Aeronautical Systems Inc., of California. Finally, the RQ-4 Global Hawk is an unarmed, high-altitude long-endurance aircraft used for surveillance. It is larger and faster, and can stay in the air longer than the Predator and Reaper. It is built primarily by Northrup Grumman, with contributions by Raytheon and L3 Comm.[4]

THE CHANGING ROLE OF THE PILOT

Drone warfare is designed to provide a greater number of flight hours per shift of ground crew, pilots, and commanders, and to increase command oversight and control over the conduct of the aircraft. Instead of the highly trained and physically fit fighter pilot, the drone pilot can work at great distance from the operational base. Because of computer guidance, the drone pilot needs far less skill, particularly at the relatively low speeds.

The pilot maneuvers the aircraft in mid-flight but ground crews direct the takeoffs and landings. The drone pilot sits in a leather chair in an air-conditioned trailer with a thrown-together and temporary feel. This could be at one of several locations: Creech Air Force Base, Nevada; Holloman AFB, New Mexico; Ramstein, Germany;[5] or even Saudi Arabia or Turkey. Along with a sensor operator, the pilot monitors video feeds and other data, and communicates with ground forces and intelligence analysts and senior officers at the stateside base or other location. The sensor operator is lower in rank than the pilot (usually enlisted), is at a work station identical to the pilot's, and even has a set of flying controls. The operators on average have more experience than drone pilots, including handling challenging flying situations. The pilots are either newer recruits, or are rated "cockpit pilots" (actual fliers) doing a rotation in a drone squadron.[6] Those analysts and command officers see what the pilot sees; the more senior commanders can provide direct authorization for hostile action.

Some of the pilot skills in takeoff and landings are now done at the forward base or by computer. Analysis of video and data and decisions on the use of force can now be made remotely as well. The drone pilot has been deskilled by the standards of twentieth-century flying. The idea that the drone pilot is a "joystick warrior," and that video game players are the pilots of the future, is an indication of how little a drone pilot will need to know to do this job. Drones are not really "unmanned" for, as Caroline Holmqvist says, they are as much a part of the human-material military system as any other relationship between people and the weapons that they direct.[7]

It appears that part of the intention of the move to Drone Nation is to transform the place of the traditional pilot in the USAF. Missy Cummings is a retired navy aviator who now teaches at MIT and directs its Humans and Automation Lab. She has been a vocal advocate of the move to drone aircraft. Cummings argues that experienced pilots may not make the best drone operators because they rely on indicators unavailable to operators working at a distance, such as wind shear on the aircraft and the "feel" of the airframe under different conditions. She has even commented that as drone warfare rises, traditional piloting skills will go into decline; the "fighter pilot mafia" will lose its control within the military.[8]

Taylorist and Fordist values are at play here as well. Taylorism, as mentioned in chapter 1, is named for Frederick Winslow Taylor, whose insight in the 1890s was that economic productivity could be greatly increased by creating more specialization among workers. He put more emphasis on the design of the industrial production process to increase management control and minimize the need for the workforce's discretion or creativity. Fordism, pioneered by Henry Ford and the Ford Motor Company, added the moving assembly line to the production process, leading again to a remarkable increase in productivity.

The application of Taylorism to piloting means dislodging the pilot as generalist and as a member of a modern version of a medieval guild. The drone pilot won't need to be in great physical condition and have strong hand-eye coordination, or understand airframes and maneuvering, takeoff and landing protocols, weaponry, the laws of war, or even the rules of engagement. Many of these attributes will be designed into computer software or allocated to senior officers "in the loop." Peter Asaro notes that internal USAF studies have identified roughly eleven distinctive tasks for each drone pilot and sensor operator. As we would expect, the studies seek to "identify inefficiencies in the labor production of drone operators and potentially to reconfigure their work practices to reduce or eliminate these inefficiencies." The military is on the record as embracing the "quality of working life" approach to human resources, so naturally is also concerned about stress in the workplace.[9]

The move to drone warfare is in part an attack on the USAF and its position that combat flight is a job for its highly educated office corps. An example of the critique is found in a military blog author named Old Soldier Colonel who advocates for the reestablishment of the army air corps, based on the argument that it allows enlisted personnel such as specialists to fly drones, instead of commissioned officers at or above the rank of lieutenant. (An army specialist is above a private first class and on the corporal pay scale but without the command authority of a corporal.) In 2012 dollars, a specialist with two years' experience earns $41,500, while an air force captain earns over twice that and a lieutenant-colonel over four times that amount. Army-enlisted personnel fly small Hunters, Shadows, and even the Sky Warrior—a UAV that is a foot longer and can carry 325 pounds more than the MQ-1 Predator. The army flies drones at a fraction of the cost of the air force, using more junior personnel with less skill and experience, and, in Old Soldier Colonel's view, has a strong case to run its own air support, and even to split all military aviation with the US Navy.

Based on Old Soldier's experience in Vietnam, the "inefficiency" of the USAF is not a new phenomenon. He recalls that in 1966 the US Army was ordered to give up its "troop carrier" fixed-wing aircraft to the USAF. The rest of his comments are worth reproducing in full[10]:

> The untold story here was when the Army was flying the C-7s, each Army Aviation Company of 24 Caribous was commanded by a Major with a captain leading each platoon of 8 aircraft and a few lieutenants but mostly warrant officers piloting the planes. When the Air Force took over, each Major was replaced by a Lieutenant Colonel Squadron Commander and each Captain platoon leader was replaced by an Air Force Major Flight Leader. The Warrant Officer pilots were all replaced by AF [Air Force] commissioned officers although several Army Warrants accepted AF Direct Commissions to keep flying them. Bottom line was, it cost the AF at least 25% more in salaries to fly the same planes doing the same missions as the Army was flying!

So the USAF not only faces rationalization pressures from the wider society, but also from other military services.

The central unit in drone warfare is referred to as the Combat Air Patrol, (CAP) and provides for the great expansion of time in the air. An official publication notes that the USAF currently has sixty-one drone CAPs with a plan to increase this number to 165.[11] The CAP's goal is to have the capability to fly one or more drones twenty-four hours a day, seven days a week. Each CAP will be assigned four drones and not all will be in the air at any one time because of refueling, rearming, routine maintenance, or more significant repairs. The pilot and sensor operator work eight- to twelve-hour shifts so two to three pairs can keep a single drone in the air for a full twenty-four hours. Similarly, there will always be a ground crew on duty at the forward base to attend to takeoffs, landings, and maintenance. Note that the link between pilot and specific aircraft has been broken. Whereas a conventional pilot can fly only so many hours a day, in part because of the physical demands of flying at high speeds, drone pilot/sensor operator teams can spend a high percentage of their workdays in flight. And while these drones are vulnerable to anti-aircraft artillery or countermeasures, they are also relatively disposable. No pilot will be lost in a drone crash, and the aircraft loss will amount to between one and twelve million dollars compared to the more than $100 million price tag of losing a cutting-edge fighter, such as the upgraded F/A-18 Hornet.

It is worth saying, too, that the current capabilities of drone warfare, embodied in the Predator, the Reaper, and the Global Hawk, are only the beginning. Without doubt, there are powerful forces behind the idea that most, if not all, of the USAF's aircraft can and should be remotely piloted, or semi-autonomous and eventually fully autonomous. Northrop Grumman is testing a drone fighter for the navy called the X-47B. According to the company, it can land perfectly every time on the pitching deck of an aircraft carrier, and its payload can be fitted for surveillance equipment, tanks for mid air refueling of other aircraft, or bombs or missiles. It has computer technology that surpasses the Automatic Carrier Landing System that live pilots can and do use. Research and development are also in process to enable drones to taxi on the carrier deck and to follow the standard arm signals of the "yellow shirt" deck crew.

And there is more. BAE Systems in the United Kingdom is developing the Taranis, a drone stealth aircraft that is invisible to radar and has intercontinental range. Boeing's Phantom Works is developing an attack fighter called the Phantom Ray. The Defense Advanced Research Projects Agency is funding research into a new ground-support drone aircraft to replace the A-10 Warthog, the "flying gun." Future mission scenarios include sending drones on high-risk missions that are too risky for live pilots, or for drones to act as wingmen to a live pilot flying in formation.[12] These aircraft fly far faster than most contemporary drones, so computer software will need to be much more advanced.

One of the current conundrums of the USAF is the relationship of *rated pilots*—qualified to fly fighters, bombers, or transports—and drone pilots who are qualified only to fly drones. In the 2000s the USAF transferred rated pilots to drone duty with a "temporary duty" designation for up to three years. Those with flying experience were considered best qualified to fly drones. Few pilots, however, want to make a permanent shift to drones because it is boring and may also be career suicide—promotion to command level seems to favor cockpit pilots. They are likely to regard flying drones as a step down, which is aggravated as the USAF increases the percentage of drone pilots who are unqualified in the cockpit. On the other hand, stories of senior officers flying drones may mean that they can finish their twenty or thirty years until pension time without riding a desk. While it is difficult to find any open admission of this, if cockpit pilots are most likely to rise to command, then it makes sense for advocates of drone warfare to get these same pilots time in the overstuffed chair. This would be a way of familiarizing and socializing cockpit pilots in drone warfare, so that as they rise up the chain of command, they will bring that familiarity with them. Using cockpit pilots as drone pilots may raise the status of flying drone aircraft.

Despite the interest in expanding drone activities, and the attractiveness of an officer's pay envelope in a stagnant economy, there continues to be a shortage of pilots. In 2010, the USAF created a new employment classification known as 18X, which is a pilot qualified to fly drones exclusively. The cost of training and time is only a fraction for that of cockpit pilots.[13] Though drone piloting can be done wearing shirt sleeves, in both the United States and United Kingdom drone pilots wear flight suits on duty. And in both countries drone pilots receive distinctive wings; the UK wings have a blue laurel wreath design to distinguish them from cockpit pilots, while in the United States the standard chevron contains a lightning bolt coming to earth.[14] As Peter Asaro puts it, drone warfare is as much "killing work" as any other job in the military,[15] so one might well ask why they shouldn't have the same regalia as others. It is an open question, however, as to whether drone pilots will stay in the program for long periods. It may be like air-traffic control careers, which are shorter than average. Drone pilots are often in the lower half of successful candidates. The best qualified candidates are selected for and want to serve in a cockpit, according to Bradley Hoagland in a Brookings Institution study.[16] Colonel Hoagland also points out that successful drone pilots have a skill set similar to an army sniper—patience, precision, and alertness—though this may make them hard to recruit, train, and retain, given the USAF's piloting culture.[17]

A report in early 2013 indicated that another challenge for recruiting drone pilots is that over a five-year period they were 13 percent less likely to get promotions from captain to major compared to cockpit pilots. It is believed that drone pilots spend so much time in front of their screens that they lack time for professional development or the training necessary for a competitive promotion file.[18] As in the private sector, the efficiency motivation has also undermined the career prospects of those who do this work. New data in late 2013 shows that, compared to 2011 and 2012, drone pilots are now being promoted to major and lieutenant-colonel at or near the same rate as cockpit pilots. This is in part because the USAF has made drone pilot training in programs such as Squadron Officer School a priority. Also the USAF has instructed promotion boards to take into account the lack of training opportunities.[19]

Information was released in August 2015 indicating that, aside from weaponized drones operated by the CIA, the US military is going to put its drone eggs in more than one basket. The plan is to accept that the USAF can't meet its commitment to run sixty-five CAPs on an ongoing basis, despite its desire to increase the number to ninety. They will run sixty CAPs and the US Army will run ten; civilian contractors will run ten (said to be mainly for surveillance), and the US Special Operations Command will run ten.[20] There is every reason to expect that the US Navy will also be in on the drone game, especially as drone carrier-based fighter-bombers become operational. This means that all three major military services will have an organizational interest in expanding and prospering the drone program with an incentive to compete for political support. Historically, this shared interest provided a guarantee that the drone program will continue to grow. The air force and navy may be under pressure to follow the army and allow nonofficers to fly drones. This is evident with the late 2015 decision to allow USAF-enlisted personnel to fly Global Hawks, the surveillance-only vehicle in the drone fleet. Experienced drone pilots were also offered a $125,000 bonus to sign on to a new five-year commitment.[21]

HEALTH AND STATUS OF DRONE PILOTS

Lambér Royakkers and Rinie van Est argue that the technology of the drone program encourages moral disengagement by the operators. They can't really be held morally responsible for what they do,[22] though this may not be the way the operators see it. According to one school of thought, drone pilots actually have a higher risk of stress and post-traumatic-stress disorder (PTSD) for several reasons. First, because drone pilots aren't required to be fit, they tend to spend a high percentage of their workday sitting in front of their screens, which leads to various health problems, including depression. Second, unlike the excitement of flying—and *pulling Gs*—the strength of the drone (its ability to circle and monitor the same scene for many hours) actually spells monotony for the pilot and sensor operator.[23] Cummings's MIT group released a study in which the second-best scores in testing drone pilots were achieved by those who were distracted some of the time. The theory is that drone pilots are more likely to be alert and engaged when they need to be if they vary activities by checking texts and e-mails, eating, or doing paperwork.[24]

Third, because the sensors and camera optics are so good, the drone pilot is more likely to see the before, during, and after of the application of force.[25] Contrast this with high-altitude or low-altitude fighter-bomber pilots, who are either so distant or moving so fast that they drop their payload and disappear from the scene of the resulting death and destruction. Once one Hellfire or other ordnance is launched, the drone pilot is likely to see the impact and may even do a "double-tap" to finish off anyone not killed on the first impact or to kill those who come to investigate or provide aid for the injured. Numerous former US military service people have spoken out in the media with similar concerns. Cian Westmoreland and Lisa Ling spoke to a hearing of the European Parliament in June 2016 in opposition to the use of weaponized drones. The United Kingdom is the only European country that has adopted weaponization but it is a subject that will be debated in other countries.[26] Westmoreland and Ling worked as technicians in the drone program and provided firsthand testimony of much of the material discussed in this chapter.

This question of whether drone pilots are really warriors is also at the heart of the controversy over the Obama administration proposal to strike a new medal in recognition of their achievements. In 2012 William Pastore commented that a new special medal for drone warfare was unnecessary because the military has a "bewildering array" of medals that it can give out; action in warfare can't really be "distinguished" when there is no risk to one's own person and no pressure from the enemy.[27] In February 2013, toward the end of his tenure, Defense secretary Leon Panetta announced a new medal called the Distinguished Warfare Medal. As the first combat medal created since the Bronze Star in 1944, it was intended to reward individuals for "extraordinary achievements" related to a military operation after September 11, 2001, but one where the individual was not in the war zone or did not risk his or her own life. It was to become the third-highest combat-related decoration, between the Silver Star and the Bronze Star.[28] This was arguably part of the effort to raise the status of drone warriors, and to signal the importance of the contribution of those regarded as immune from the wounds of war.

The response to this announcement was largely negative. Groups such as the Veterans of Foreign Wars argued that no medal for performance in "the rear" should be ranked higher than medals awarded to those in harm's way, such as the Purple Heart and the Bronze Star.[29] Despite claims that the

Secretary, the Joint Chiefs, and key people supported the decision, and that this would not be the first medal that ranks above combat medals,[30] it took only two months for new Defense secretary Chuck Hagel to announce its cancellation.[31] He instructed officials to come up with a proposal for a pin, clasp, or other device that could be applied to medals and decorations. But by early 2014 the Pentagon announced an overall review of all medals and decorations. A year later the Obama administration decided to award an *R* decoration (for remote) to be attached to other medals as a means of recognizing drone pilots.[32]

A future concern will be how the move to semiautonomous and possibly fully autonomous drones affects human culpability. David Axe reports that the military worries that drone pilots may either feel too much or too little responsibility for their actions, though no doubt the former concern is the greater one. In her research, Cummings has administered personality tests, finding that "conscientiousness" is the most important characteristic for this low-task-load environment, but notes that drone pilots "may also hesitate when the time comes to fire a weapon."[33] Consider that drone pilots work standard shifts and then go at home at night to their families, making them the first generation of US warriors who fight in distant lands but do not live in or near the war zone. Further, drone warriors live in a world of diluted responsibility because of the role of sensors and the sensor operator, communication with ground forces, and the fact that offensive action is likely to be approved only by higher-ups.

This can also be complicated because of a diversity of voices providing direction for drone pilots and sensor operators, voices that can operate with different military rules of engagement. It has been known for a long time that some US drones are under the direction of the Pentagon while others are under the direction of the CIA with its "theater of operations" likely to be mainly Pakistan. It has also been assumed that CIA drones are piloted by CIA officials under different rules compared to the military. However, it has become increasingly clear that military units, such as the 732nd Operations Group at Creech AFB, Nevada, have been contracted to fly drones under CIA orders.[34] If it is possible to contract out military jobs to civilians, then surely it is possible for intelligence operations to be contracted to the military. A problem for drone pilots is that CIA orders will come through a different process and, not surprisingly, with less concern for the specific rules and restrictions codified in USAF procedures. Drone pilots serve different masters at different times, each with a different rule book. This is bound to cause some adversity for the pilots, particularly if there are lethal consequences for people on the receiving end of the strikes.

The robot for search-and-rescue drones may be designed to look human. This can provide comfort to the victim and also allow others to attach credit or blame depending on how things go. Research on offensive military drones is moving toward two-way voice communication in order to anthropomorphize the drone so that the human operator can deflect some of the responsibility onto the software.[35] If an operator can talk to the drone and the drone can talk back, the drone pilot's culpability will be reduced, thus avoiding situations such as that of a drone pilot named Brandon Bryant, who resigned from the military because it was clear to him that he killed a child as "collateral damage,"[36] despite official denials and reassurances.

CONCLUSION

It appears that the rise of drone warfare provides an opportunity for the "brass" in the US military to break the power of cockpit pilots. They have found a new form of labor that is easier to monitor and control, and that will not have the autonomy that pilots have enjoyed since the beginning of human flight early in the twentieth century. The military is seemingly a great employer in terms of compensation and benefits, even in a stagnant economy. Yet this chapter also raises the possibility that in an environment of permanent and unpopular war, the military can't meet its recruiting or retention targets for what are literally "cushy positions." This does not bode well for the future of the US military given the emphasis on drone warfare. And if the US military advances plans to expand the use of drones and to cut compensation for drone pilots, its current challenges may worsen considerably. Beyond recruiting and retraining, the military also needs to deal with mental health issues because of everything from moral disengagement, culpability, and diluted responsibility from serving two masters—the military and the CIA.

NOTES

1. Steve Niva, "Disappearing violence: JSOC and the Pentagon's new cartography of networked warfare," *Security Dialogue* 44(3 [2013]): 185–212.
2. Jeremy Packer and J. Reeves, "Romancing the Drone: Military Desire and Anthropophobia from SAGE to Swarm," *Canadian Journal of Communication* 38 (2013): 309–31.
3. Derek Gregory, "From a View to a Kill: Drones and Late Modern War," *Theory, Culture and Society* 28(7–8 [2011]): 188–215, esp. 205.
4. Bill Yenne, *Birds of Prey: Predators, Reapers and America's Newest UABs in Combat* (North Branch, MN: Specialty Press, 2010), 152–53. For a children's book on the predator, see Michael and Gladys Green, *Remotely Piloted Aircraft: The Predators* (Mankato, MN: Capstone Press, 2004).
5. "US operates global drone war from German base—ex-pilot," *Russia Today*, April 6, 2014.
6. James Dunnigan, "Pilots Despise Flying UAVs," Strategy Page, August 30, 2012, https://www.strategypage.com/dls/articles/Pilots-Despise-Flying-UAVs-8–30–2012.asp .
7. Caroline Holmqvist, "Undoing War: War, Ontologies and the Materiality of Drone Warfare," *Millennium: Journal of International Studies* 41(3): 535–52, esp. 545.
8. Michael Milstein, "*Pilot Not Included: Military aviation prepares for the inevitable," *Air and Space Magazine*, July 2011.

9. Peter M. Asaro, "The labor of surveillance and bureaucratized killing: New subjectivity of military drone operators," *Social Semiotics* 23(2): 196–224.

10. Old Soldier Colonel Blog, "Drones—UAVs—RPVs: The Argument for Why They are the Future of Military Aviation and Who Should be Flying Them!" August 5, 2012, http://old-soldier-colonel.blogspot.ca/2012/08/drones-uavs-rpvs-argument-for-why-they.html.

11. Chris Carroll, "Unmanned now undermanned: Air Force struggles to fill pilot slots for drones," Stripes, August 25, 2013, http://www.stripes.com/news/unmanned-now-under-manned-air-force-struggles-to-fill-pilot-slots-for-drones-1.236906.

12. Milstein, see note 8 above.

13. The material in this paragraph is drawn from Dunnigan, see note 6 above.

14. Lewis Page, "RAF graduates first class of new groundbased 'pilots'" *The Register*, April 4, 2013, http://www.theregister.co.uk/2013/04/04/raf_drone_rpas_pilots_graduate/.

15. Asaro, see note 9 above, 202.

16. Bradley C. Hoagland, *Manning the Next Unmanned Air Force: Selecting the Pilots of the Future*, (Washington, DC: Brookings Institution, 2013), 13.

17. Ibid., 5.

18. Agence France-Presse, "US Air Force Lacks Volunteers to Operate Drones," August 21, 2013.

19. Jeff Schogol, "More unmanned aircraft pilots being promoted," *Military Times*, November 6, 2013.

20. CBS News, "Pentagon planning more drone usage over next several years." August 17, 2015, http://www.cbsnews.com/news/pentagon-planning-more-drone-usage-over-next-several-years/.

21. Kelsey Atherton, "Air Force Will Let Enlisted Pilots Fly Global Hawks: An old lesson in manpower learned anew," *Popular Science*, December 21, 2015, http://www.popsci.com/air-force-will-let-enlisted-pilots-fly-global-hawks.

22. Lambér Royakkers and R. van Est, "The cubicle warrior: The marionette of digitalized warfare," *Ethics and Information Technology* 12 (2010): 289.

23. Mark Thompson, "Drone Pilots: No Worse Off Than Those Who Actually Fly," *Time*, April 2, 2013.

24. Jennifer Chu, "Driving drones can be a drag: Study shows distractions may alleviate boredom and improve drone operators' performance," November 14, 2012, http://phys.org/news/2012-11-distractions-alleviate-boredom-drone.html.

25. James Dao, "Drone Pilots Are Found to Get Stress Disorders Much as Those in Combat Do," *New York Times*, February 22, 2013.

26. Alice Ross, "Former US drone technicians speak out against programme in Brussels," *The Guardian*, July 1, 2016, https://www.theguardian.com/world/2016/jul/01/us-drone-whis-tleblowers-brussels-european-parliament.

27. William Astore, "The Drone Medal," Huffington Post, July 13, 2012, http://www.huffingtonpost.com/william-astore/the-drone-medal_b_1671481.html.

28. Lolita C. Baldor, "Pentagon Creating New Medal For Drones, Cyberattacks," February 13, 2013, http://www.spokesman.com/stories/2013/feb/14/pentagon-creating-new-medal-for-cyber-drone/.

29. Jason Lomberg, "Do drone pilots deserve higher medal than combat vets?" February 20, 2013, https://www.ecnmag.com/article/2013/02/do-drone-pilots-deserve-higher-medal-com-bat-vets.

30. Bryant Jordan, "DoD Stands behind Controversial Drone, Cyber Medal," February 20, 2013, http://www.military.com/daily-news/2013/02/20/dod-stands-behind-controversial-drone-cyber-medal.html.

31. Baldor, "U.S. Defense Secretary cancels new military medal for drone and cyber warriors," *National Post*, April 16, 2013.

32. Atherton, "Pentagon Agrees to Recognize Drone Pilots with a Decoration (Not quite a medal)," *Popular Science*, January 7, 2016.

33. Chu, see note 24 above.

34. Chris Woods, *Sudden Justice: America's Secret Drone Wars* (Oxford and New York: Oxford University Press, 2015), 16.

35. David Axe, "How to Prevent Drone Pilot PTSD: Blame the 'Bot," *Wired,* June 7, 2012.

36. Henry Blodget, "U.S. Drone Pilot Explains What It's Like When You Realize You Just Killed a Kid," *Business Insiders*, May 13, 2013.

Chapter Five

Drones for Corporate Profit and Domestic Surveillance

Star Simpson, Dustin Boyer, and Scott Torborg, of Silicon Valley in California, have a dream. It's well known that technology developed and perfected for military use often later finds applications in civilian life, whether it's contemporary plastics or the Internet. So if drone aircraft do such a great job in conflict zones throughout the world, then why not allow them to be used for civilian, commercial purposes within the United States, and eventually other countries? Drones are already being used by members of the US border patrol, by civilian police departments, and by firefighters. Whether at home or abroad, surely drones can do work that might be described as "dull, dangerous, or dirty." And their use is particularly attractive given that the purchase price and operating costs are only a fraction of that of full-size helicopters and airplanes.

Domestic use of drones, however, does raise unavoidable questions of privacy and safety. Polls are showing citizens are concerned about domestic surveillance and how information gathered could be used against them. And drone technology is not considered completely safe in terms of possibilities of midair collisions, standards of training, and the aircraft's vulnerability to sabotage.

But not all domestic applications have the seriousness or weight of security protection, or other issues, which is where Simpson, Boyer, and Torborg come in. They have launched an Internet startup called TacoCopter.com, and their dream is to use small drone aircraft to deliver tacos to customers. In the words of *Huffington Post* contributor Jason Gilbert, this concept combines "the most prominent touchstones of modern America: tacos, helicopters, robots and laziness."[1] The idea is that customers over a large geographic area use their smartphone to order and pay for one or more tacos. Their location would be available via GPS data, and the Tacocopter would be dispatched to drop its tasty payload. This could be done without a delivery person and at a very competitive cost. Of course, as Gilbert writes, even enthusiasts for the idea recognize there are numerous barriers, such as "navigating the treacherous terrain of an urban environment, keeping the food warm, finding a city map precise enough to avoid crashes 100 percent of the time, avoiding birds, balconies and telephone wires, delivering food to people indoors, delivering food to the right person, [and] dealing with greedy humans who would just steal the Tacocopter as soon as it got to them." The kicker is that as of mid-2012 the Federal Aviation Administration (FAA) would not license the Tacocopter, and as company founder Simpson commented, "it's a little bit ironic that that's the case in a country where you can be killed by drone with no judicial review."[2]

BEYOND TACOS

The principals of TacoCopter.com better move quickly or else they will be left in the rotor wash of events. The first case of a domestic delivery by an unarmed drone has already been executed. Australian startup Flirtey, in collaboration with NASA and Virginia Tech, delivered ten pounds of medical supplies from a rural Virginia airfield to a medical clinic a mile away after a three-minute flight. Amazon, Google, and Facebook are working on commercial drone technologies either to service their core businesses (particularly in the case of Amazon), or to diversify their business.[3]

While these may seem like trivial examples, one of the great challenges of the next few years, particularly for activists who want to "uncool" drones and prevent their normalization in domestic life, will be the degree to which drones will be permitted to enter national civilian airspace. Apart from the questions of public safety, there are widespread concerns about how domestic drone operations may eliminate the possibility of privacy from government or corporate surveillance. It should be no surprise that the financial stakes are large for advocates of a domestic role for drone aircraft, since by 2020 there could be thirty thousand drones in the air as part of a market that amounts to $12 billion in sales each year.[4] There is a Congressional Privacy Caucus, but there is a much larger Congressional Drone Caucus. And so far, the drone caucus is winning.

One of the concerns about the widespread use of drones in combat is that they will be acquired by every country, making everyone vulnerable to attacks because of the small size and perceived difficulty of intercepting them. But another worry is that there will be great pressure to allow drones, increasingly popular technology, to be used for domestic civilian purposes without much regard for the consequences. The first step was taken in February 2012 when on a bipartisan basis Congress reauthorized the FAA, providing it with legislative priorities and direction in exchange for its annual budget.[5] The legislation contains little known provisions directing the FAA to clear the way for widespread domestic drone use by 2015. The provisions are worth summarizing briefly, as available information is vague or contradictory.

In section 332, within 270 days of its passage the Secretary of Transportation is directed to produce a "comprehensive plan" to "safely accelerate the integration of civil unmanned aircraft systems into the national airspace system." The contents of the prospective plan are defined, and within one year of passage the secretary must make public a five-year roadmap for the introduction of drone aircraft for civilian purposes. By mid-2014 the secretary is directed to publish rules—to take effect December 31, 2015—on the domestic integration of drones, considering experimental projects, and their use in parts of the Arctic under US sovereignty. Section 334 provides that starting in 2012 there be an expedited process to allow drone use by universities, and federal, state, and municipal governments and agencies. They must weigh up to twenty-five pounds and operate within the operator's line of sight, below four hundred feet off the ground, during daylight, and five miles outside aviation activities such as airports.

In 2012, twenty-five universities possessed certificates allowing drone use, largely for R and D, rather than on-campus snooping. While domestic drones are sold officially for surveillance purposes, some reports say that there are off-the-record discussions between police departments and Texas-based Vanguard Defense Industries, for example, about weaponizing drones, such as with grenade launchers and 12-gauge shotguns.[6] It is worth noting that the language of "shall" is used in the federal statute, so that the FAA and Transportation Department are not able to rule out the domestic use of drones. One could say that Congress and the President have decided in principle that drones will soon fly domestically.

From the vantage point of 2016, the FAA has made good on these legislative mandates. Commercial operators such as Amazon have been waging a fierce lobbying campaign, arguing that they will develop "sense-and-avoid" technology that will make restrictions unnecessary; so far there has been no change.[7] In June 2016 the FAA released its initial 624-page rule book, and the limits on drone use indicate that the federal government has been forced to respond to some of the public criticism. Drones must be flown in daylight, no higher than four hundred feet, within sight of the operator or a forward observer; operators much be sixteen years or older and must also pass a written aeronautical test and be recertified every two years.[8] It is not yet clear how the key issue of personal privacy will be regulated.

Despite the balance of forces behind domestic drone use, resistance is now manifest, beginning with public opinion. In a 2012 national poll with a sample size of 1,700, respondents were asked whether they support or oppose the use of drones for various law-enforcement purposes. Results are telling: 27 percent claimed that they knew "a great deal" about unmanned surveillance aircraft used by the military, while 29 percent said they knew "some" and 44 percent said they knew little or nothing. On the use of drones in search and rescue, 80 percent said they were in support, while 67 percent said they supported using drones to track runaway criminals. A slightly smaller number, 64 percent, said they supported using drones to control illegal immigration, while only 23 percent said they supported using drones to issue speeding tickets.

PRIVACY CONCERNS

Fully 64 percent of poll respondents were very or somewhat concerned about protection of their own privacy "if US law enforcement started using unmanned drones with high tech cameras."[9] In July 2012, citing privacy concerns, ranchers and lawmakers in the Midwest protested the fact that the Environmental Protection Agency was using drone aircraft to identify water, land, and air pollution.[10]

It is very likely that people have something to worry about. Writing for the Congressional Research Service, staff legislative attorney William M. Thompson II made a strong claim in support of allowing surveillance information in court, particularly if the drones exist for a purpose other than law enforcement. "Unless a meaningful distinction can be made between drone surveillance and more traditional forms of government tracking, existing jurisprudence suggests that a reviewing court would likely uphold drone surveillance conducted with no individualized suspicion when conducted for purposes other than strict law enforcement."[11] Even if the law requires a warrant, Thompson believes the courts will defer to law enforcement when it comes to information that "happens to come into their possession" from drones that are deployed for some other purpose, such as commerce or protection of health and safety. This is the means through which governments will be able to access even greater information about the population, including targeted individuals.

A 2015 report in *Wired* magazine noted that drones can simulate cell towers if they are positioned correctly and have access to cell-phone usage in particular areas. The author also said that if drones are to be used at the country's borders, then they should be restricted to within ten miles. They should also not be weaponized, the rules should be transparent, and there should be certainty that the benefits exceed the costs.[12]

Where public opinion goes, pundits and politicians are not far behind. On the political right, Charles Krauthammer and Anthony Napolitano said on

Fox News in May 2012 that there is enough opposition to domestic drone use that a red-blooded American who shoots one down is likely to be widely celebrated. As Krauthammer put it, "The first guy who uses a Second Amendment weapon to bring a drone down that's been hovering over his house is going to be a folk hero in this country." Napolitano repeated the same message soon after, though in his case he didn't say he was just making a prediction.[13] If one needs role models, one can find on the Internet videos of people showing *how* to shoot down drones. Alex Jones, known for advocating conspiracy theories on subjects such as what really brought down the Twin Towers on 9/11, is featured with "the Steiner brothers" shooting down commercial drones like skeet and explaining why it's important to be ready to do so.[14] On the political left, there is also a growing literature critical of both foreign and domestic drone use, often found on websites such as *Alternet, Counterpunch, The Intercept, TomDispatch and Truthout,* as well as in popular books such as Medea Benjamin's *Drone Warfare: Killing by Remote Control.*

Politicians on both sides of the aisle have also begun to express their dissent through legislative proposals. On June 12, 2012, Senator Rand Paul (R-KY) introduced the "Preserving Freedom from Unwarranted Surveillance Act of 2012" (S. 3287), with two cosponsors, Senators Coburn of Oklahoma and DeMint of South Carolina. Paul's one-page bill says that the federal government or those bodies it funds are not permitted to use drone aircraft to gather evidence in federal investigations unless a warrant is obtained in advance.[15] Paul is remembered for his March 2013 filibuster in the Senate on the issue of the use of drones and assassination of American citizens. The companion legislation in the House of Representatives (H. R. 5925) was introduced by Rep. Austin Scott (R-GA), with the support of twenty cosponsors. While there is no sign that either of these bills will come to a vote in the foreseeable future, they have provoked the beginning of congressional interest, including hearings designed to highlight the issues.

On the Democratic side, then-representative Ed Markey of Massachusetts, cochair of the Congressional Privacy Caucus, released the "discussion draft" of a proposed law in late July 2012. It is a longer and much more ambitious effort to limit and regulate the domestic use of drones. The legislation requires that the Secretary of Transportation study the ways in which domestic drone use may compromise privacy; that FAA rules be written to protect personal privacy; that agencies licensed to use drones articulate how their drone use will avoid violating personal privacy; that the licensee establish policies to destroy data unrelated to the purpose for which the drone is licensed; that there be public disclosure by the FAA of licenses granted and for what purpose; and that licensees obtain a judicial warrant for general surveillance "without a particular target." It also grants the power to enforce the law to the Federal Trade Commission and provides a role for civil actions in the US District Courts.[16] Markey's proposals echo the concerns raised by staff of the Electronic Privacy Information Center in various forums.[17]

SAFETY PROBLEMS

While these legislative initiatives have not made it into law, and at this point may not even come to a vote in either of the legislative chambers, they have provoked congressional hearings which in themselves are interesting and raise awareness. On July 18 and 19, 2012, the Subcommittee on Oversight, Investigations and Management of the House Committee on Homeland Security held hearings on the domestic use of drone aircraft. Many witnesses pointed to problems. The most general discussion, focusing on safety and other technical issues, was offered by Gerald Dillingham, the director of Physical Infrastructure Issues for the US government's General Accountability Office. He pointed out that under existing rules, the FAA had issued 201 certificates of authorization for domestic drone use to 106 public agencies at the federal, state, and municipal level in the previous six months alone.[18]

Dillingham raised alarms over problems that have not been successfully addressed and that will loom large should greater numbers of drones be permitted within US airspace. First, he noted, there is no sense-and-avoid technology that would help drones avoid midair collisions.[19] Because there is no pilot in the drone, and the operator's viewing angles are limited, there should be proximity alerts so that the drone can avoid collisions. For example, the website Defense Tech reported on August 17, 2011, that a small RQ-7 Shadow drone collided with a US MC-130 Hercules transport plane in Afghanistan. Photos accompanying the article showed significant damage to the front of the transport's left wing, but the Hercules landed safely.[20]

Second, aviation security may be compromised because of the problem of gaps in "uninterrupted command and control."[21] There are numerous cases, both military and civilian, in which the drone operator has effectively lost control of the drone because of a disrupted communication link. Richard Conniff, writing in *Smithsonian* magazine, noted that in late 2010 a Northrop Grumman Fire Scout experienced a "lost link" and ventured into restricted airspace in Washington, DC, before the operator regained control.[22] Such breaks in communication are common. In a case like this they can endanger life and property if they crash or if they are shot down as a perceived risk to high-value targets.

Third, Dillingham says that a problem of drone use is the question of "standards of performance and training."[23] Given the ease of takeoff, landing, and use, how will drone piloting standards be enforced? Who will train users? Will the resources and enforcement be available to ensure that standards are consistently met? Finally, he commented that because current FAA regulations don't account for drone aircraft, a great deal of work will be necessary to amend these regulations. The *Washington Post* reported in June 2014 that there were forty-nine domestic crashes of military drones from 2001 to 2015 and over four hundred internationally. There is reasonable concern that civilian domestic drones will also be as, or more, susceptible to this type of failure.[24]

In a recent article, Nick Turse argues that the technology that drone advocates point to with such enthusiasm is a long way from coming to pass.[25] While the drone arsenal in the US military has expanded greatly in recent years—from ninety in 2000 to 9,500 in 2012—most of these drones do surveillance rather than act as a platform from which attacks are launched. Turse points out that drones are vulnerable to crashes, sabotage, poor weather, and enemy attack. As he says, "Even the Predator and the Reaper are little more than expensive, error-prone, overgrown model airplanes remotely 'flown' by human pilots. . . . Even the Reaper is slow, clumsy, unarmored, generally unable to perceive threats around it and—writes defense expert Winslow Wheeler—'fundamentally incapable of defending itself.'"[26] Turse believes that remotely controlled drones—let alone futuristic autonomous vehicles—are likely to suffer from glitches that limit their effectiveness over the long term. A report in the *Washington Post* notes that according to the UN, US drones have had numerous near-misses in Somalia. Their presence may be in violation of the UN's arms embargo applied to Somalia since 1992. According to the UN, there were sixty-four unauthorized flights of drones, fighter jets, or attack helicopters in Somalia in one year starting in June 2011.[27] Writing in *Slate*, Brian Palmer commented that despite Pakistan's public objections to US drone flights, it takes no action because it chooses not to; the larger, armed drones, like the Reaper and Predator, appear on radar, fly at only one hundred miles per hour, and are easy targets for Pakistani fighter pilots.[28]

Increasing drone presence in US domestic air space, and that of other countries, may well have a transformative impact. North Dakota now permits law enforcement to outfit drones with Tasers and rubber bullets, and it may only be a matter of time before they can mount more lethal ordnance. How this came about is also instructive, for once it comes into law in one state it becomes normalized and extended to others. Rep. Rick Becker introduced a bill that required the police to have a warrant to use a drone for surveillance, though as Gregory Ferenstein tells it, "then local law enforcement managed to sneak in the right to equip drones with Tasers or rubber bullets by amending the original prohibition against lethal and non-lethal force to just limiting lethal weapons."[29] Weak government and part-time legislators, with few or no professional staff, greatly strengthen lobby organizations. Representatives like Becker, whose day job is as a plastic surgeon, have a hard time keeping up with, let alone staying ahead of, well-funded organizations with strong legislative preferences.

As law enforcement considers weaponizing domestic drones, it need only look to the innovations being pioneered by civilians. In the summer of 2015 a video went viral on the Internet, showing the work of an eighteen-year-old student in Clinton, Connecticut, who rigged a drone with a semiautomatic handgun and then fired it on remote command. The student's family also made public a video showing a flamethrower attached to a drone immolating a Thanksgiving turkey. Law enforcement said it might only be illegal if the firing happened within municipal boundaries.[30] By 2016 the FAA decided to investigate these two incidents, and the family is in federal court trying to quash a subpoena on the grounds that a hobby drone is not an aircraft and therefore cannot be regulated by the FAA.[31] In March 2016, *USA Today* wrote that a report by the inspector-general of the Department of Defense, released under federal access to information legislation, indicates that on twenty occasions Pentagon drones were loaned for lawful civilian purposes over the previous ten years. According to the Pentagon the drones provided assistance mainly for floods, fires, search and rescue, and assisting with "National Guard exercises."[32] In a world where transformations happen via baby steps, these domestic uses of military drones can be expanded over time.

Todd Humphreys, a University of Texas at Austin engineering professor, testified in the Homeland Security Committee hearings discussed above on the relative ease of "spoofing" the GPS signals that civilian drones rely on. It is not well known outside of technical circles, but there are two GPS signals accessible in the US—an encrypted one for the military, and one for civilians for which there is "clear access." Humphreys recounts working cooperatively with the Department of Homeland Security to show how it is possible to crash a civilian drone by spoofing its GPS signal and taking over control of the craft.

Humphreys and his students constructed a "GPS spoofer" that allowed them to interfere with the internal guidance of a Hornet Mini, an $80,000 rotorcraft. While he did not go into great detail, Humphreys explained that the equipment sends a GPS signal at low power, and then by raising the power the spoofed signal "takes over" as the dominant signal for the drone. By changing the GPS signal, the operator of the spoofing equipment can simulate a "rise" in the drone's altitude. If the drone is set to hold steady at a certain altitude, then the drone (or the human operator) will take corrective action to reduce its height. A significant change will cause the drone to crash. Humphrey says that this spoofing technology is not available to the "ordinary person on the street," although persons with engineering and physics training can develop them. "There is no quick, easy, and cheap fix for the civil GPS spoofing problem. What is more, not even the most effective GPS spoofing defenses are foolproof," he says.

Humphreys suggests that civilian drones of eighteen pounds or more be required to have spoof-resistant navigation systems, and that Homeland Security fund the development of a cryptographic authentication system for civilian GPS.[33] Lorenzo Franceschi-Bicchierai of *Wired* magazine reports that even the unorganized can undermine GPS signals: "In late 2009, GPS receivers at Newark Airport were going down intermittently every day and no one understood why. It took two months to track down the source of the interference: a driver had installed in his truck an illegal GPS jammer— which can easily be bought online for $50—so that his employer couldn't track his every move. In 2001, a boat's television antenna preamplifier took out GPS over the entire harbor town of Moss Landing, just south of San Francisco, for weeks."[34]

More recently, IBM employee Nils Rodday told a conference that while he was a graduate student at the University of Twente, Netherlands, he came to an arrangement with a commercial quadcopter manufacturer to reverse-engineer the drone's security and try to crack it. He signed a nondisclosure agreement and cannot reveal the firm or model, but said it was easy to hack the $30,000–$35,000 drone. Rodday took away control from its proper controller from a distance of up to a mile. He says the encryption is weak despite the fact that these drones are used by police and other government agencies. He suspects that these problems may be widespread.[35]

Though still in the dawning of the drone age, creative people have picked up on the vulnerability of drones, generating many ways to undermine them in their civilian, police, and military manifestations. With tongue firmly in cheek, the creative people behind the website downwithdrones.com generated no fewer than fifty-two ways to bring down drones, including slingshots, bow and arrow, boomerangs, and other traditional weapons; catapults, arbalest, trebuchet, bolo, and other medieval-sounding contraptions; bubble-generating machines, silly string, high-energy radio frequency guns, tennis balls, rocks, casting fishing rods with hooks, medium-range paintball pellets, aerial trip wires, kites and balloons with fishing lines, throw nets, and radio-controlled hobby planes (as counter-drones).[36]

"Hacktivists" are starting to think about how they can use drones to undermine the state and corporate establishments, support citizen journalism, expose ecological crimes, protect the Occupy and similar social movements, and eavesdrop on both audio and electronic communications.[37]

It is worth saying that the authorities are also working on technology to limit what domestic drones can do, or to prevent rogue drones from being part of terrorist plots or other offensive actions. Government and private-sector scientists are working on software that will prevent drones from coming within a certain distance of domestic airports. They are also working on microwave technology that will force aggressive drones back to their user and allow the authorities to pinpoint and apprehend the humans in control.[38] CBS News reported in the summer of 2015 that the Department of Homeland Security alerted all law-enforcement agencies of the risks of domestic drone attacks.[39]

CONCLUSION

While most of the public discussion and media coverage has been about the military uses of drones, all evidence suggests that domestic drones are shaping up to have a transformative impact on everyday life in the United States. And when other countries have military drone capabilities, domestic use will be common throughout the world as well. Domestic drones can be used in nonviolent ways by government and can prove to be useful in anything from fighting crime to fighting forest fires. The technology can even be used to create commercial opportunities for taco-loving citizens! As explained in this chapter, however, privacy is a serious and growing concern. Technological glitches and the ability to spoof GPS signals combine to make domestic use something to be wary of. At the same time, positive uses by citizen groups are in the works. Drone manufacturers and advocates are likely to be in the "long game," and will be content to make only gradual progress toward their ultimate goal of free rein for domestic drone aircraft around the world.

NOTES

1. Jason Gilbert, "Tacocopter Aims to Deliver Tacos Using Unmanned Drone," Huffington Post, March 23, 2012.
2. Ibid.
3. Edd Gent, "The Future of Drones: Uncertain, Promising and Pretty Awesome," Livescience.com, November 5, 2015, http://www.livescience.com/52701-future-of-drones-uncertain-but-promising.html.
4. "The drone over your backyard: A guide," *The Week*.
5. FAA Modernization and Reform Act of 2012, 112th Congress, Public Law 95, http://thomas.loc.gov/cgi-bin/bdquery/z?d112:h.r.658.
6. Jefferson Morley, "Drones for 'urban warfare,'" *Salon.com*, April 24, 2012.
7. David Morgan and D. Seetharaman, "Industry lobbyists take aim at proposed FAA drone rules." Reuters, February 23, 2016, http://www.reuters.com/article/us-usa-drones-lobbying-idUSKBN0LS04R20150224.
8. Bart Jansen, "FAA completes landmark rules for commercial drones," *USA Today*, June 21, 2016, http://www.usatoday.com/story/news/2016/06/21/faa-commercial-drone-rules/85641170/.
9. Evan Ackerman, "Poll Shows Concern about Drones and Domestic Surveillance," IEEE Spectrum, June 25, 2012, http://spectrum.ieee.org/automaton/robotics/military-robots/poll-shows-concern-about-drones-and-domestic-surveillance.
10. David Pitt, "Midwest ranchers, lawmakers protest EPA flyovers," Huffington Post, July 2, 2012.

11. William M. Thompson II, "Drones in Domestic Surveillance Operations: Fourth Amendment Implications and Legislative Responses," *Congressional Research Service*, April 3, 2013, 17, http://www.fas.org/sgp/crs/natsec/R42701.pdf.

12. Thor Benson, "Five Ways We Must Restrict Drones at the US Border," *Wired*, May 20, 2015, http://www.wired.com/2015/05/drones-at-the-border/.

13. "Anthony Napolitano and Charles Krauthammer on domestic surveillance drones," *Slate.com*, May 16, 2012.

14. Paul J. Watson, "Surveillance drones blasted out of the sky in protest against 4th amendment intrusion," Infowars.com, May 29, 2012, http://www.infowars.com/drones-shot-down-over-texas/.

15. US Congress, "Preserving Freedom from Unwarranted Surveillance Act of 2012," S. 3287, 112th Congress, 2nd session, June 12, 2012.

16. Andrea Stone, "Drone Privacy Bill Would Put in Safeguards on Surveillance," Huffington Post, August 2, 2012.

17. Amie Stepanovich, Electronic Privacy Information Center, "Testimony and Statement for the Record," submitted to the Subcommittee on Oversight, Investigations, and Management of the House Committee on Homeland Security, July 19, 2012.

18. Gerald L. Dillingham, "Unmanned Aircraft Systems; Use in the national airspace system and the role of the Department of Homeland Security," United States Government Accountability Office, July 19, 2012.

19. Ibid., 5.

20. "Midair Collision between a C-130 and a UAV," *Defense Tech*, August 17, 2011.

21. Gerald L. Dillingham, "Unmanned Aircraft Systems; Use in the national airspace system and the role of the Department of Homeland Security," United States Government Accountability Office, July 19, 2012.

22. Richard Conniff, "Drones are Ready for Takeoff: Will unmanned aerial vehicles—drones—soon take civilian passengers on pilotless flights?" *Smithsonian*, June 2011.

23. Gerald L. Dillingham, "Unmanned Aircraft Systems; Use in the national airspace system and the role of the Department of Homeland Security," United States Government Accountability Office, July 19, 2012.

24. Craig Whitlock, "Crashes mount as military flies more drones in U.S.," Pt. 2, *Washington Post*, June 22, 2014, http://www.washingtonpost.com/sf/investigative/2014/06/22/crashes-mount-as-military-flies-more-drones-in-u-s/.

25. Nick Turse, "A Drone-Eat-Drone World," *Z Magazine* XXV (7/8): 55–58.

26. Ibid., 56.

27. Whitlock, "Drone operations over Somalia post danger to air traffic, UN report says," *Washington Post*, July 24, 2012.

28. Brian Palmer, "Is It Hard to Kill a Drone? *Slate*, June 6, 2012.

29. Gregory Ferenstein, "Weaponized Drones for Law Enforcement Now Legal in North Dakota," *Forbes*, August 25, 2015, http://www.forbes.com/sites/gregoryferenstein/2015/08/26/weaponized-drones-now-legal-inside-the-u-s-lawmaker-says-crimefighting-will-become-a-video-game/#77ee93e37a57.

30. Michael Martinez et al., "Handgun-firing drone appears legal in video, but police, FAA probe," CNN, July 21, 2015, http://www.cnn.com/2015/07/21/us/gun-drone-connecticut/.

31. Jason Koebler, "Teen Fights to Defend His Legal Right," *Motherboard*, June 7, 2016, http://motherboard.vice.com/read/teen-fights-for-the-right-to-strap-guns-to-drones.

32. Gregg Zoroya, "Pentagon report justifies deployment of military spy drones over the U.S.," *USA Today*, March 9, 2016, http://www.usatoday.com/story/news/nation/2016/03/09/pentagon-admits-has-deployed-military-spy-drones-over-us/81474702/.

33. Todd Humphreys, "Statement on the Vulnerability of Civil Unmanned Aerial Vehicles and Other Systems to Civil GPS Spoofing," Submitted to the Subcommittee on Oversight, Investigations, and Management of the House Committee on Homeland Security, July 18, 2012.

34. Lorenzo Franceschi-Bicchierai, "Drone Hijacking? That's Just the Start of GPS Troubles," *Wired*, July 6, 2012.

35. Andy Greenberg, "Hacker Says He Can Hijack a $35K Police Drone a Mile Away," *Wired*, March 3, 2016, http://www.wired.com/2016/03/hacker-says-can-hijack-35k-police-drone-mile-away/.

36. No author, http://downwithdrones.com/.

37. Sabine Blanc, "Drone Activism Takes to the Sky," OWNI.EU, March 13 2012. See also the account of "Telecomix," a French hacker collective that is building drones and other high-technology devices to help Syrian anti-government activists, http://globalfree.wordpress.com/tag/drones/.

38. Reuters, "U.S. Government, Police Working on Counter-Drone Measures," Newsweek.com, August 20, 2015, http://www.newsweek.com/us-government-police-working-counter-drone-measures-364453.

39. Jeff Pegues, "Homeland Security warns drones could be used in attacks.," CBS News, July 31, 2015, http://www.cbsnews.com/news/homeland-security-warns-drones-could-be-used-in-attacks/.

Chapter Six

Influential Opinions

Think Tanks and Pundits

The United States was meant to be a republic. The 1787 Constitution declared that property-owning men were citizens, with all powers in their hands unless granted to local, state, or national government. This definition of citizens was broadened over the succeeding two hundred years to include men without property, women, African Americans, and other excluded groups. The Constitution and its Amendments continue to define and limit the power of governments versus the people. There are many elected offices, especially compared to the British-style Westminster limited monarchy in which the voter elects only one officeholder, the local member of Parliament.

In the original vision of the American republic, election is the chief means through which the voter directs policy making and lawmaking. Those elected are expected to have real power. Add to this the Constitution, a complicated interaction of central political institutions and a federal system designed to diffuse rather than centralize government power. It was accepted that there would be divisions of opinion, referred to by James Madison as "faction," but this would be managed by the representative nature of the system and the division of powers; no one faction should be able to attain complete power. This system was accepted by the American people in part because a number of writers intervened in the public discourse in advocacy of the new model through what is known as *The Federalist Papers*. Arriving in Philadelphia in 1789, they were educated men but they were not professors, intellectuals, or "policy wonks," as we now think of them, and they were certainly not paid "talking heads."

It is no surprise that the independent opinion leader did not survive nineteenth-century events like westward expansion, civil war, major population growth, industrialization, and urbanization, or America's twentieth-century rise to superpower status.

This chapter is about the role that experts such as journalists, editorialists, pundits, academics, and think-tank scholars play in the realm of the international and domestic use of drones. It is inevitably informed by "the elephant in the room," as the performance of the vast majority of these experts over the last fifteen years has been dreadful, specifically in connection to 9/11, the US war in Afghanistan and invasion of Iraq, and activities in Libya and other countries in North Africa, the Horn of Africa, and the Middle East. While the next chapter examines the role of the media, the issue overlaps here as think tanks and pundits use the media as their public platform.

US print and broadcast media, with a few notable and noble exceptions, largely discredited themselves and led to the mass departure of their audience to Internet sources and alternative forms of information, including *faux* news like *The Daily Show* and *The Colbert Report*. Greg Mitchell's book, published in 2008 and with a title that says it all—*So Wrong for So Long*—is a useful reminder of the breakdown of the chattering classes. It would take a 747 to transport those who failed. To scratch the surface of Mitchell's list we find William F. Buckley, Jr., Ann Coulter, Thomas Friedman, Francis Fukayama, Jim Hoaglund, David Ignatius, William Kristol, Chris Matthews, Mary McGrory, Dan Rather, Joe Scarborough, George Will, and Bob Woodward. Those who got it right, like Amy Goodman, Chris Hedges, Norman Solomon, and Jon Stewart, can be carried in a much smaller conveyance.

The classic idea is that there is a "marketplace of ideas" featuring those whose ideas are the best product. What is remarkable, as Mitchell says, is that "few of those who promoted the war based on false information have lost any standing in the media, even if they did lose respect from some in the audience."[1] And those who got it right are still only seldom found on corporate television or other media.[2]

THE POWER OF THINK TANKS

It is telling to outline the rise and role of think tanks, their sheer number, and the conditions under which they can be independent. Conflict of interest, nondisclosure of interests, and the role of donors is also vital to discuss. Think tanks may add to the debate but also sow doubt or confusion and they dull conclusions on policy issues simply by the information they release. This is especially true regarding weaponized international and domestic drone use. The domination of pro-drone opinion in the media and think-tank universe can explain, in part, public acquiescence to drone warfare as well as domestic drone use. It is, however, worth noting that think tanks do produce material that departs from official government policy, even when they are government sponsored.

Developments in the last forty years are quite remarkable, not only because of the change in journalism but also the rise of full-time pundits drawing salaries from tax-exempt organizations. This began in the 1960s with the breakdown of the society-centered "pluralist model," and the rise of alternatives.[3] *Neopluralism*, for example, sees the consistent domination by one set of social forces or interest groups. *Instrumental Marxism* sees one class in control of the state, inspired by Marxist thought. *Structural Marxism* theorizes that the state will act to maintain the capitalist system even against the short-term wishes of the ruling bourgeois class. And *democratic elitism* claims that elitist control of politics is inevitable and desirable, especially in a complex, urban industrial society. One could also add a cross-cutting theory inspired by the German sociologist Max Weber that challenges the society-centered account. It offers instead that government or the state is at the center of American life and that the idea of citizen or social control of government is an illusion.

This also appears to be the same period when there is either a change in the effectiveness of voting, or, more likely in this account, a change in the realization of the actual significance of voting. It has been increasingly obvious that replacing the party in power does not even make a marginal difference in policy and law. At all levels, winning the election is only the beginning of the process. Those who are elected have a mandate—their liberty and obligation—to implement their platform. But despite great differences during the campaign, governance does not reflect diversity of opinion.

Fast forward to the 1970s. By then Americans were accustomed to the lobbyist, that representative of industry, labor, students, gun owners, or other interest groups, who tries to influence legislation through providing meals, travel junkets, and bribes. The most legal and cleanest form of influence had been campaign contributions to enable reelection. But the number of think tanks has exploded. As Thomas Medvetz says in his important book on the subject, think tanks are not very easy to define, which perhaps provides them with their potency. He points out that the historical discussion over their rise has been dominated by pluralist and elite theorists, those inheritors of the debate over the very nature of the US political system. For pluralists, think tanks are like any other organization in that they enter the "empty arena" or "marketplace of ideas" and compete for the policy outcomes they want. For elite theorists, the rules of the game are already rigged and only those think tanks that square with elite interests can have any real impact. One might also add that neopluralists, or some of those in the Marxist tradition, would see think tanks, like lobbying organizations, as part of the fight but with an outcome that is not as predetermined as elite theorists would have it.

Medvetz brings this description of think tanks' influence to the table: "the products of a long-term process of institutional growth and realignment, have become the primary instruments for linking political and intellectual practice in American life." Further, he argues that "any intellectual figure who wishes to take part in American political debate must increasingly orient his or her production to the rules" of this system. The think-tank system "has undermined the value of independently produced knowledge in the United States by institutionalizing a mode of intellectual practice that relegates its producers to the margins of public and political life."[4] The great task of congressional committee staff and leadership, and the media, is deciding who to book for the testimony, television show, or print interview, since that will determine the direction of the discussion or the design of the debate. This leads us to predict that the lone intellectual from the "University of X" is less and less likely to get a hearing without a think-tank affiliation. This is reinforced by the changing university in which the typical professor has increased teaching, research, and service expectations, and therefore does not have time to intervene in public debates. Those who have the luxury of being public intellectuals probably have a "course buyout" from a think tank!

The importance of lobbyists and think tanks is connected to the transformation of US politics. Unlike the classic formulation, the election is not the end of the consultative process. After the election, the diverse forces with an interest in politics *relitigate* the issues (to use President Obama's term) in front of decision makers, in public and private, regardless of the election outcome. What those decision makers will ultimately do is very much in the hands of major donors and investors who can make or break political leaders and even the US economy. We are now in an era of the *deep state*, to use a term made prominent by former Republican political staffer Mike Lofgren,[5] in which policy continuity election after election is ensured by the continuous process of political donations. Policy is facilitated and justified by the wide range of think tanks that serve both dominant and insurgent interests— those in power, out of power, and nowhere near power. As William F. Grover explains, it is misleading to ask whether a president has an expansive or restrictive view of government. Rather, the president, up to and including Obama, is the "'chief stabilizer' of political and economic order in the United States."[6] Notwithstanding the Bernie Sanders and Donald Trump insurgencies during their dramatic 2016 campaigns for the White House, forces in favor of continuity now greatly outweigh forces for change, with experts and think tanks at their service. This is a challenge for capitalist libertarians, libertarian socialists, Tea Party members, and Occupy supporters. From G. William Domhoff's perspective, think tanks are a major part of what he refers to as the "policy-planning network," which is a predominant but not omnipotent force in the making of policy and explaining policy continuity.[7]

The number of think tanks is mindboggling. There are 1,989 think tanks in North America with 1,830 of these in the United States. This outnumbers Europe, which hosts 1,822, though together North America and Europe have 60 percent of the world total. More than half of these are university-affiliated. A whopping 90.5 percent of all think tanks were created since 1951, and the number in the United States has more than doubled since 1980. Around one quarter of US think tanks (about four hundred institutions) are in Washington, DC, which suggests some business with, or dependence on, the federal government. Importantly, the number of new think tanks has declined over the last eleven years,[8] no doubt connected to stagnant economic times and perhaps to a sense that for every purpose a think tank already exists.

A general definition according to James McGann[9]:

> Think tanks are public-policy research analysis and engagement organizations that generate policy-oriented research, analysis, and advice on domestic and international issues, thereby enabling policymakers and the public to make informed decisions about public policy. Think tanks may be affiliated or independent institutions that are structured as permanent bodies, not ad hoc commissions.

Perhaps those who can claim independence will have the most credibility in an age of suspicious readers and viewers. In reality, almost everyone is dependent on someone, apart from the tenured academic doing pure research with an unlimited, ironclad grant of academic freedom, a secure salary, and either guaranteed funding or no need for funding. McGann suggests that we classify think tanks as "Autonomous and Independent," Quasi-Independent," "Government Affiliated," "Quasi-Governmental," "University Affiliated," "Political Party Affiliated," and "Corporate Affiliated (For Profit)."[10] As we will see, it does not matter a great deal whether these think tanks operate within government, within universities, or are free-standing. All are capable of generating research that narrowly serves those who fund or direct it, or they can act in an independent-minded fashion if their sponsors desire.

Further light can be shed on the role of think tanks within powerful institutions by looking at past insights into the role of secretariats and think-tank equivalents in the UN system. For many decades, including before the rise of think tanks in domestic politics, scholars of international organization, now called "multilateralism," have asked about the decision-making processes in inter-governmental organizations (IGOs). In theory the state members of IGOs have the *power*, shared with the appointed leader of the secretariat, to make decisions and steer the organization. However, there are many individuals within the organization who have *influence*, as was pointed out by Robert Cox and Harold Jacobson in their pioneering work on the subject.[11] Further, in every organization there is an establishment—that senior collection of staff who act as the "consensus-minded group." They are the ones "whose function is to reconcile views among the various divergent elements within the organization, to place limits on conflict, and to aggregate policy at the higher levels of the organization itself."[12] This may seem rather obvious, as internal workings of organizations are no longer seen in monolithic terms. It took a long time, however, for scholars to come to now-commonplace conclusions regarding internal diversity within organizations.

As Cox points out in his later work, it is possible that there will be units within an IGO that are permitted, or even encouraged, to work at cross-purposes from the organization's main goals. As he wrote in 1979, "One way in which an established institution can ward off the risk of arteriosclerosis and mental atrophy is to harbor in its midst a ginger group of critics whose acknowledged role is to challenge policy orthodoxy, to redefine issues, and to propose alternative methods of dealing with them. The International Institute for Labour Studies [IILS], founded within the framework of the [International Labour Organization] in 1960, might have performed a role of this kind."[13] The autonomy and functions of the internal think tank wax and wane over time, according to what is permitted by bureaucratic or political forces. This remains true today: just because a think tank exists within a corporation or government does not mean that it slavishly follows either; rather it may be *counter-hegemonic*, to use the Gramscian term. It may be set up to promote a certain case that the political leadership of the corporation or the government cannot advocate for political reasons.

THOSE WITH AUTHORITY

McGann helps us answer the question of which think tanks are regarded as the best or most influential. His organization surveyed 20,000 university administrators and academics, journalists, think-tank scholars, executives, and donors from around the world, of which 3,572 responded. He also relied on 1,950 functional and regional experts, and he invited the participation of over 6,500 think tanks. The top seven think tanks are described as prestigious, long-standing, and not hyperpartisan or hypersectarian, with the partial exception of the Center for Strategic and International Studies (CSIS). The others are the Brookings Institution, Carnegie Endowment for International Peace, Council on Foreign Relations, Woodrow Wilson International Center for Scholars, RAND Corporation, and Pew Research Center. More tendentious organizations on the list are the Cato Institute, the Heritage Foundation, and, on the other side of the spectrum, the Center for American Progress.[14] There is a broad mix of think tanks among the top sixty, though conservative and libertarian organizations outspend, outnumber, and generally outrank more liberal ones. Perhaps they have more to achieve given the resistance of voters across the spectrum to revolutionizing public policy. This is exemplified by their resistance to domestic "entitlement reform," a major think-tank preoccupation.

Think-tank donors receive significant influence over research and advocacy. In October 2014, Project Censored made this its eleventh most under-reported story for the previous year. They wrote that in the United States there is no requirement that think tanks reveal their funding sources, even though contributions are tax-deductible. They also pointed out that oil companies and weapons manufacturers are major donors to the country's leading think tanks. It is even possible to channel money to organizations like the DonorsTrust Foundation which then passes it to the intended recipient with little chance of the contribution being traced. [15] There is also concern that foreign governments are funding US think tanks and putting pressure on employees to advocate for those governments' interests. In September 2014 Brooke Williams published a piece in the *New York Times* in which she identified the Brookings Institution, CSIS, and the Atlantic Council as three bodies that have accepted foreign donations that have shaped their research program. She traced $92 million that has come into the United States mainly from Europe, the Middle East, and Asia. But think tanks are not considered lobby organizations and face less government regulation than do lobbyists. [16]

Sometimes pundits will be selected because they are making a case on behalf of a government that doesn't want to publicly support a particular position. A good example is an opinion piece produced by Seth G. Jones of the RAND Corporation in December 2009. In "Take the War to Pakistan," he argues that the United States should not make the same mistakes the Soviets made in Afghanistan, which was to think they could win without going after Taliban/al Qaeda safe havens in Pakistan. [17] (At the risk of a tangent, it is refreshing that a commentator has suggested that the United States needs to learn from the Soviet experience, since by implication the United States is in the same type of enterprise as the Soviets. This is not an idea for mass consumption!) To intervene in Pakistan he advocated police/intelligence operations and drone strikes. The Obama administration was doing this very thing as he wrote, even if it was denying it publicly. Jones's piece can be seen as an effort to persuade opinion leaders of the merits of a secret policy that has been implemented via the CIA. It's not that Jones or any other pundit is necessarily tailoring his or her ideas to suit the administration or other powerful actors; rather, the ideas meet with the approval of decision makers and ends up on the *New York Times* opinion page.

Think tanks can also act as enforcers for certain views, enlisting their prestige in the effort. On October 14, 2012, *New York Times* public editor Margaret Sullivan wrote a critique of *Times* coverage of drone warfare, specifically the question of labeling civilians as militants. She said the paper has not "aggressively challenged the administration's description of those killed as 'militants'—itself an undefined term." This was too much for Benjamin

Wittes, senior fellow in Governance Studies at the Brookings Institution, who described the column as "very weird" in his Lawfare blog. He wrote: "The Times is not an advocacy organization whose job it is to 'aggressively challenge' the government's claims of the rates of civilian casualties—except to the extent that those claims are untrue."[18] As Glenn Greenwald pointed out in a subsequent column in praise of the original Sullivan piece, "The only way to find out whether government claims are untrue is by aggressively challenging them. A failure to do so ensures that even the most dubious and unproven of government assertions go unchecked."[19] One would have thought that a believer in the First Amendment to the Constitution would defend the press's right to skepticism about government, especially in light of the dreadful performance of establishment media and think tanks over the last fifteen years that led the United States into disastrous wars of aggression. While Greenwald is not known for pulling his punches, Wittes's earlier position, taken before this incident, was that he would not engage with Greenwald because of his "pervasive suggestion in his work of the corruption and ill-motive of his opponents, whom he serially fails to credit with believing the arguments they are making" and because he treats those who don't agree with him as operating "in bad faith, are on the take, or are evil."[20]

We do not know if Greenwald has ever addressed this in his voluminous writings but there is an important point to be made here. It is something that Wittes and many others coming from an individualistic perspective do not understand. It is not that they do not believe what they are saying. No doubt it is preferable that they believe it because they are less likely to slip up or recant. But they are where they are and have the platform they do because of what they say. The mainstream media in the United States offers an incredibly narrow range of opinion (compared to Europe and the global South). Greenwald started by publishing in *Salon* and the UK *Guardian* but his ideas are spread through the underculture of the Internet, mainly through his current platform *The Intercept.* That is the fate that awaits anyone with his views.

The think-tank world is not much better, heavily weighted to the interests of advertisers, donors, and the private capitalist economy. The debate for and against drone warfare, assassination, and the kill list often plays out in the hands of rival think tanks. For example, writing in 2012 in the venerable *Foreign Affairs*, Christopher Swift, a fellow at a university-based think tank in Virginia, argues that based on research in Yemen, drone strikes have not been a successful recruiting tool for al Qaeda in the Arabian Peninsula.[21] No doubt part of his goal, as a supporter of drone warfare, is to undermine the argument that killing people via drone strike (or other bombing) tends to recruit more soldiers for the enemy cause.

A meeting point of the role of experts, punditry, think tanks, and uncritical media is captured in the case of Gen. Jack Keane, a senior military commander in the George W. Bush era. He is retired and now leads a think tank called the Institute for War Studies. As Lee Fang wrote in *The Nation* in 2014, when Keane is interviewed in the media he invariably advocates militaristic solutions to global problems and US reentry into countries like Iraq. At best the media refer to him as a retired general and leader of a think tank; little else is said about what he is currently doing. His think-tank partners include neoconservative militarists Liz Cheney and William Kristol. As the author says, Keane's other activities are:

> special advisor to Academi, the contractor formerly known as Blackwater; as a board member to tank and aircraft manufacturer General Dynamics; a "venture partner" to SCP Partners, an investment firm that partners with defense contractors, including XVionics, an "operations management decision support system" company used in Air Force drone training; and as president of his own consulting firm, GSI LLC. To portray Keane as simply a think tank leader and a former military official, as the media have done, obscures a fairly lucrative career in the contracting world. For the General Dynamics role alone, Keane has been paid a six-figure salary in cash and stock options since he joined the firm in 2004; last year, General Dynamics paid him $258,006.

Fang also notes that this same conflict-of-interest analysis applies to many other Washington talking heads, including Gen. Anthony Zinni and former Homeland Security advisor Frances Townsend.[22]

One of the most important public-policy think tanks, and one with a decided point of view, the American Legislative Exchange Council (ALEC) was founded in 1973. It is conservative/libertarian, funded by entities like Koch Industries and has a reputation for drafting and distributing right-wing model legislation that undermines trade unions, environmental regulation, government deficit financing, and tax increases. Rob Schofield of NC (North Carolina) Policy Watch notes that ALEC has taken an interest in domestic drone use. He points out that some of the elected officials in North Carolina who are working on pro-drone legislation have ties to the defense industries and the ALEC committees.[23] He also cites specific ALEC documents, though as of this writing they have disappeared from the ALEC website. The one drone reference there, however, is to a pro-domestic-drone opinion piece in the *Richmond Times-Dispatch* by Jon Russell, a Culpeper, Virginia, town councillor who described himself as a founder of the "American City County Exchange." This organization appears frequently on the ALEC website, a hint that it is a front organization, an idea reinforced by Russell's e-mail address ending in alec.org.[24]

The Heritage Foundation's views on drones are interesting because they take a distinctive position, but one that can be explained. In their 2013 backgrounder, Steven Groves takes a pro-weaponized-drone position similar to other conservative views. He argues that the United States should not back off from its position; that the country has the authority under the laws of war and inherent right to self-defense "to target and suppress threats to US national security wherever they may be found"; that the September 2001 AUMF should not be weakened; and that "Congress and the Administration should reject calls to establish a judicial or quasi-judicial 'drone court' to scrutinize the targeting decisions made by US military and intelligence officers."[25] The Foundation is far more restrained on the domestic use of drones. Instead of favoring commercial interests, as some conservative/libertarian organizations do, it takes a strong constitutional and civil liberties perspective supporting great restrictions. It also supports the principle of *posse comitatus*, that the US military not be used domestically.[26]

In the realist tradition in foreign policy and international relations, the border of an ordered state represents a fundamental dividing line. The territory outside is a disordered area in which the *law of the jungle* prevails, whereas all that is within is civilized, ruled by domestic law. This thinking is a reflection of the ongoing influence of Hans Morgenthau and his followers in the United States, and the English School in the United Kingdom. English School member Martin Wight claimed in a famous 1960s essay that there is "political theory" and there is "international theory," but there is no political theory of the world outside the state. He believed that "international society has been so organized that no individuals except sovereign princes can be members of it," and that "every individual requires the protection of a state, which represents him in the international community."[27] There are no citizens of the world in that traditional vision; there should be no expectation of civilized treatment outside of the state. For the Heritage Foundation the United States is a well-ordered state with Constitution, Bill of Rights, and rule of law. Different rules apply outside, including so-called failed states. And one of those rules allows overflights and attacks by drone aircraft. As Chatan Bhatt has written, there is a contemporary obsession with the security risks of "ungoverned space"[28] in the Obama administration. This major concern justifies the explosion of drone warfare.

SOWING DOUBT, OBSCURING FACTS

Judging from the history of the debate over climate change, as well as previous controversies, one of the goals of the funders of think tanks is simply to sow doubt in public opinion. While winning the debate is desirable, creating doubt is acceptable because it means decision makers don't face a backlash for doing what fossil-fuel producers want—to allow the oil and fossil-fuel economy generally to continue at full blast regardless of the consequences. In the case of drone warfare, the result of doubt was to allow decision makers to retool the military toward remote killing and permanent war.

As Naomi Oreskes and Erik Conway point out, over the last number of decades there have been several scientific controversies in which a minority of contrarians challenge virtually unanimous scientific opinion at the behest of powerful economic forces wanting to ensure market-oriented solutions and weak government (except when strength is needed by business interests). Based on major donations from right-wing actors, bodies like the George C. Marshall Foundation (1984) were created to deny the scientific consensus. They consider key cases over the last several decades as the health effects of direct and indirect tobacco smoke, acid rain, Soviet military superiority, Reagan's SDI, and global warming. The pattern has always been the same. Even after there is a scientific consensus, they make several claims: that there is a lack of clarity or consensus, that nothing needs to be done, or that something is to be done on a "free-market basis." This generally means that only the sovereign consumer or investor is permitted to solve the problem, given the absence of government regulatory action.[29]

The Soviet military superiority/SDI case, like drone warfare, illustrates that this is really about corporate funders in league with militaristic policy makers calling the shots. It is not about minimal government or free enterprise at all. The purpose of conservative foundations was to convince the inattentive public that all the technological promises were true. SDI technology would work to identify, target, and destroy Soviet missiles, thus rendering them useless. Another task was to assure people that they should not be concerned that SDI would be a decisive, first-strike weapon, even though the postwar nuclear balance of power (i.e., deterrence) was based on mutual assured destruction. The victim would have the capacity to retaliate, thus deterring the nuclear power contemplating the first strike. SDI was of course the proper term for the product, whereas Star Wars smacked of the fantasy of "long, long ago in a galaxy far, far away."

The fact that people talk about climate change instead of global warming was a win for the conservative think tanks, because climate change is less specific; climate is not just changing, but global temperatures are getting warmer. If targeted killing sticks instead of assassination or murder, this would also be a think-tank win. Targeted killing bears the assumption that this killing is like any other in war, no doubt unfortunate, but part and parcel of what happens when people commit aggression against us. The term *drone* is also not first-rate as a brand label from the perspective of some of its advocates, as discussed earlier. Most important for them is that people believe that twenty-four-hour drone coverage and camera optics mean that the United States knows who it is killing, mistakes are not made, and collateral damage is minimized. At least the goal is for people to be uncertain about it, because if people are arguing about this they aren't arguing about whether the country should even be actively fighting in Pakistan, Iraq, Syria, Afghanistan, Yemen, Somalia, Libya, and so forth.

In a 2013 *Alternet* column David Sirota amplifies this. His starting point is a comment from Senator Angus King (I-ME) who said that drone warfare involves the use of a "humane weapon" because it is allegedly precise and minimizes the harm done to civilians compared to larger-scale bombing or introduction of US troops. But moderate and conservative drone supporters don't want people to realize that military de-escalation and withdrawal is another option worth discussing. As Sirota says:

> In a country whose culture so often (wrongly) portrays bloodshed as the most effective problem solver, many Americans hear this now-ubiquitous drone-war argument and reflexively agree with its suppositions. Having been told in so many ways that killing is the best and only possible policy prescription, most simply assume that our only national security choice is between drone wars and ground wars—between different forms of pre-emptive violence, and nothing else.[30]

While not total victory, keeping the discussion within narrow boundaries is certainly a partial win.

A related role of think tanks is to soften up conclusions by introducing new data to obscure what is going on. This is similar to the dynamics of "triangulation," that skill of successful Democrats or Republicans to make decisions not based on platform or principle, but on a precise reckoning of where to land on a multidimensional policy spectrum. They need to preserve the political and financial support of the partisan base, while at the same time undermine and attract neutral and opposition support. This is exemplified by the competitive counting of alleged militant and civilian deaths from US drone strikes by the Bureau of Investigative Journalism (BIJ) and the New America Foundation (NAF). The higher BIJ figures are most widely quoted in the media. This happens in front of a larger societal background, one in which US government officials and opinion leaders are either indifferent toward civilian deaths of the "other" or deny or seek to minimize those deaths. This is not a new phenomenon but rather goes back centuries, John Tirman argues.[31]

The official discourse about drone attacks is undermined if it turns out that innocent civilians are regularly being killed. On the surface the NAF appears to be a solid source of information and not a militaristic mouthpiece. It is led by Steve Coll, a contributor to *New Yorker* magazine, and by Chair of the Board Eric Schmidt, chair and CEO of Google. Its major drone-policy guru, with the title of Director, National Security Studies Program, is Peter Bergen, whose work is cited elsewhere in this book. Many of its financial contributors appear to be moderate to liberal, such as the Pew Charitable Trusts and the Catherine and John D. MacArthur Foundation. These are the kind of donors who also support the Public Broadcasting System (PBS).[32] Some also appear to be on the more conservative side of the Democratic

Party, or bipartisan, such as the Bill and Melinda Gates Foundation, and the Peter Peterson Foundation[33] with its obsession with government deficits and debt.

The effect of the NAF is to provide comfort to those who look for lower casualty numbers and assurance that the Obama administration has been effective in tightening up processes to minimize civilian deaths. For example, a report by the Human Rights Institute at Columbia University Law School said that in 2011 the NAF and the Long War Journal (LWJ) both undercounted civilian deaths in Pakistan, while the minimum and maximum ranges offered by the BIJ was more accurate. Specifically, the report says that:

> Our recount found reports of between 72 and 155 civilians killed in 2011 Pakistan drone strikes, with 52 of the reportedly civilian dead identified by name—a relatively strong indicator of reliability. By comparison, New America Foundation's count is just 3 to 9 "civilians" killed during this period; Long War Journal's count is 30 civilians killed.[34]

This means that the other bodies accepted Obama administration claims and reproduced data to support that. Writing in *The Atlantic* in 2012, Conor Friedersdorf critiqued Bergen's claims on CNN, based on the work of the NAF, that civilians killed that year in Pakistan plummeted to zero.[35] Friedersdorf says that NAF data discounts Pakistani media and on-the-ground sources and relies too much on unnamed government officials and intelligence operatives. Bergen also attributed the change to new policies implemented by the Obama administration, which could be an explanation that would be approved by the White House and Democratic Party.[36] We see that Bergen's work is also approvingly cited by more conservative commentators, such as Tom Rogan in the *National Review*, thereby providing respectable cover.[37] Since no one seems to be without a think-tank home, as of this writing Rogan is Tony Blankley Chair for Public Policy and American Exceptionalism at the Steamboat Institute, Steamboat Springs, Colorado.[38]

Even if the NAF and LWJ data are greeted skeptically, it can be used to generate lower averages than the minimums and maximums produced by the BIJ. The main purpose of William Saletan's article in *Slate* is to argue that the civilian casualty rates in drone warfare are lower than in conventional bombing. He cites data from all three sources (BIJ, NAF, and LWJ) because the low numbers of the latter two reduces the average number. At the least, it casts doubt on exactly how many civilians are killed by drones.[39] In July 2016 the Obama administration issued an executive order to place greater emphasis on avoiding civilian deaths and also established that there will be disclosure of the civilian death count by the US government. Predictably, however, the administration continues to come in on the low side estimating civilian deaths of a minimum of sixty-four and maximum of 116 from 2009 to June 2016, while the LWJ says 212, the NAF says at least 219, and the BIJ says at least 325.[40]

As critics note, some of the issues that have been identified for years have not gone away. Marcy Wheeler comments that the Obama administration is only providing global figures and not numbers for each attack so that it is impossible to determine whether every incident is acknowledged. For example, a Human Rights Watch report says that a US attack in December 2009 on Al-Majalah, Yemen, killed fourteen al Qaeda fighters but also forty-two civilians. Since the United States has never admitted that it was involved in this strike, these numbers are unlikely to be part of their official tally. Wheeler says that the United States also did "side-payment" strikes for the Pakistani government (as part of the deal to allow the United States to operate freely in the "tribal areas") so it is not known whether those strikes are being counted.[41] Further, while the administration says that it is not claiming that all military-aged boys and men killed in attacks are considered militants unless later investigation proves otherwise, it still appears that the numbers reflect the policy that tends to inflate militant deaths compared to civilian deaths.[42]

A VARIETY OF VIEWS

It should be no surprise that there is a wide range of views on the question of drone warfare—approaching the Tower of Babel! American citizens, however, do not seem very concerned perhaps because of the bromides offered by think-tank policy experts as well as the mainstream media's indifference to counterevidence. Not all think tanks take extreme pro-drone positions. The Stimson Center, named for Henry L. Stimson, who served both Democratic and Republican presidents as secretary of state and secretary of war, describes itself as offering "pragmatic solutions" to global problems. In June 2014 it released a report by a ten-person panel chaired by Gen. John P. Abizaid (US Army, Ret.) and Rosa Brooks, taking a middle-of-the-road position on the weaponization of drones, warning of the risks of permanent war and urging greater safeguards in identifying targets and authorizing strikes.[43]

Writing for the Center for Strategic and Budgetary Assessments in 2014, former US Navy undersecretary Robert Martinage argued that the United States needs to continue to develop drone technology to stay ahead of rivals, such as the MQ-4C Triton. His work was also endorsed by Rep. Randy Forbes, a Virginia Republican on the House Armed Services Committee. The suggestion is that new drone technology is affordable because of savings from base closures, a reduction in the troubled F-35 fighter program, and/or a reduction of an aircraft carrier/carrier group.[44] Obviously, there would be winners and losers if this was implemented, even from within the military production constituency.

Two studies by the RAND Corporation and a think tank within the British Ministry of Defence illustrate another role for think tanks, which is to work on technical problems. In one RAND study, the authors' task is to model what the next medium-altitude drone should look like, in the context of production ending on the MQ-1 Predator, and the MQ-9 Reaper being ready for upgrading or replacement. The report provides some actual discussion (not for wide circulation) of the limitations of the drone aircraft, particularly in weather, and steps that can be taken to address these issues.[45]

Another RAND study, produced in 2006, late in the George W. Bush era, addresses the history, law, and prudence of preemptive and preventative attacks in US policy. Karl Mueller et al. provide a sober look, giving one the impression that this report, part of a larger research program known as Project Air Force, was commissioned in part as the "revenge of the strategists" versus elected and appointed "chickenhawks" in the White House and Pentagon. The authors correctly point out that preemptive attack under certain restrictive circumstances is good law and good policy (e.g., their bombers are in the air). Preventative attack is typically not legal and certainly risky strategically, politically, and on the ground—even for the world's lone military superpower. The central message? As the authors write:

> In order to provide the necessary capabilities, military planners must know what their political leaders intend with respect to anticipatory attack, with far more specificity than is provided by broad policy statements such as the National Security Strategy. Senior military officers need to keep national decision makers familiar with the extent and limits of their capabilities, particularly if pre-emptive options are going to be considered in conditions where the time available for making strategic choices is limited.[46]

They write largely from a power politics (i.e., realist) perspective, but it is the more sober, restrained version, aware of the limits of even the superpower, as compared to the more headstrong, overconfident version common among extreme neoconservatives.

An example of a think tank within government is the Development, Concepts and Doctrine Centre of the British Ministry of Defence. In 2014 it produced the fifth edition of its report entitled *Global Strategic Trends - Out to 2045*. It does not present an overly happy scenario and certainly is not the stuff of politicians' optimistic stump speeches. This is a world of considerable uncertainty, in which most states find themselves less powerful and less likely to act unilaterally. They have diverse domestic populations with all the attendant risks and rewards, with climactic fallout from global warming and the continuing rise of China politically, economically, and militarily. The authors make no mention of drone warfare, but rather anticipate technological advances in the targeting and power of laser and particle beam weapons. They also foresee biological warfare including targeting adversaries based on their DNA.[47] This sounds like the stuff of science fiction but is a peek into what is happening in research labs.

CONCLUSION

The research in this chapter makes it clear that there has been an explosion in the number of think tanks in recent years, especially in the United States. Their political viewpoints vary, but the majority lean to the right. In a world of effective electoral systems, think tanks would mostly provide interesting, entertaining commentary but be largely ignored. Instead, think tanks are part of the postelection jockeying for policy outcomes, and like other sources of punditry, the track record of the majority on security issues in the last fifteen years has been poor. There has been a long tradition of think tanks and other pundits acting at the behest of well-heeled forces, seemingly with the goal of supporting the status quo or of creating doubt about particular policy issues, ensuring stalemate and inaction. Think tanks in the United States have become an important part of maintaining public opinion in favor of current policy on drone warfare. They should think harder.

NOTES

1. Greg Mitchell, *So Wrong for So Long* (New York and London: Union Square Press, 2008), 9.

2. It goes without saying too, that people like Noam Chomsky and others with similar views have been the equivalent of "banned" from the media—to use the old apartheid South African term, albeit banned without government action.

3. For more on these theories, see G. W. Domhoff, *Who Rules America?* (New York: McGraw Hill Education, 2014), chap. 9.

4. Thomas Medvetz, *Think Tanks in America* (Chicago: University of Chicago Press, 2012), 7.

5. Mike Lofgren, *Deep State* (New York: Viking, 2016).

6. William Grover, "Deep Presidency: Toward a Structural Theory of an Unsustainable Office in a Catastrophic World—Obama and Beyond," *New Political Science* 35 (3 [2013]).

7. Domhoff, *Who Rules America?* 74–75. See note 3 above.

8. James G. McGann, "Go to Global Think Tank Index Report, Think Tanks and Civil Societies Program (TTCSP)," University of Pennsylvania, 2015, 10.

9. Ibid., 8.

10. Ibid., 10.

11. Robert Cox and H. Jacobson, *The Anatomy of Influence: Decision Making in International Organization* (New Haven, CT: Yale University Press, 1974), 399–400.

12. Ibid., 406.

13. Cox, "Labour and Hegemony," see note 11. Cox was himself director of the IILS from 1965 to 1972.

14. McGann, "Think tank index report," 74–75.

15. Project Censored, "11. Wealthy Donors and Corporations Set Think Tanks' Agendas," October 1, 2014.

16. Democracy Now, "Think Tanks as Lobbyists," September 8, 2014.

17. Seth G. Jones, "Take the War to Pakistan," *New York Times,* December 3, 2009, http://www.nytimes.com/2009/12/04/opinion/04jones.html?_r=0.

18. Benjamin Wittes, "Very Strange Column by the *New York Times* Public Editor," Lawfare, October 15, 2012, http://www.lawfareblog.com/very-strange-column-new-york-times-public-editor.

19. Glenn Greenwald, "The Brookings Institution demands servile journalism," *The Guardian,* October 15, 2012, http://www.theguardian.com/commentisfree/2012/oct/15/drones-brookings-media.

20. Wittes, "Why I Won't Engage Glenn Greenwald," Lawfare, January 16, 2011, http://www.lawfareblog.com/why-i-wont-engage-glenn-greenwald.

21. Christopher Swift, "The Drone Blowback Fallacy," *Foreign Affairs,* July 1, 2012, https://www.foreignaffairs.com/articles/middle-east/2012–07–01/drone-blowback-fallacy.

22. Lee Fang, "Who's Paying the Pro-War Pundits?" *The Nation,* September 16, 2014, https://www.thenation.com/article/whos-paying-pro-war-pundits/.

23. Rob Schofield, "Legislative committee on drones: Yet another ALEC-inspired front for industry?" The Pulse (NC Policy Watch), January 21, 2014, http://pulse.ncpolicywatch.org/2014/01/21/legislative-committee-on-drones-yet-another-alec-inspired-front-for-industry/.

24. For the ALEC link, see J. Russell, "When crafting drone policies, context is key," http://www.alec.org/russell-richmond-times-dispatch/.

25. Steven Groves, "Drone Strikes: The Legality of U.S. Targeting Terrorists Abroad," The Heritage Foundation, April 10, 2013, http://www.heritage.org/research/reports/2013/04/drone-strikes-the-legality-of-us-targeting-terrorists-abroad.

26. Paul Rozenweig et al., "Drones in U.S. Airspace: Principles for Governance," The Heritage Foundation, September 20, 2012, http://www.heritage.org/research/reports/2012/09/drones-in-us-airspace-principles-for-governance.

27. Martin Wight, "Why is there no International Theory?" in *Diplomatic Investigations: Essays in the Theory of International Politics* (London: George Allen and Unwin Ltd., 1966), 20–21.

28. Chetan Bhatt, "Human Rights and the Transformation of War," *Sociology* 46(5 [2012]), 822.

29. Naomi Oreskes and E. Conway, "Global Warming Deniers and Their Proven Strategy of Doubt," Environment 360, June 10, 2010, http://e360.yale.edu/feature/global_warming_deniers_and_their_proven_strategy_of_doubt/2285/.

30. David Sirota, "It's Just Shocking What the Drone War Cheerleaders Are Willing to Say Out Loud," Alternet, February 4, 2013, http://www.alternet.org/world/its-just-shocking-what-drone-war-cheerleaders-are-willing-say-out-loud.

31. John Tirman, *The Deaths of Others* (Oxford and New York: Oxford University Press, 2011), especially chaps. 1 and 2.

32. For information on the NAF, search the Center for Media and Democracy's source-watch.org for "New America Foundation."

33. For information, see http://pgpf.org/.

34. Chantal Grut and Naureen Shah, *Counting Drone Strike Deaths,* New York: Human Rights Clinic, Columbia University, 2012, 5.

35. For the original claim, see Peter Bergen and J. Rowlands, "Civilian casualties plummet in drone strikes," CNN, July 14, 2012, http://www.cnn.com/2012/07/13/opinion/bergen-civilian-casualties/.

36. Conor Friedersdorf, "Flawed Analysis of Drone Strike Data Is Misleading Americans," *The Atlantic,* July 18, 2012, http://www.theatlantic.com/politics/archive/2012/07/flawed-analysis-of-drone-strike-data-is-misleading-americans/259836/.

37. Tom Rogan, "In Defense of Drones," *National Review,* October 21, 2013, http://www.nationalreview.com/article/361720/defense-drones-tom-rogan.

38. http://steamboatinstitute.org/what-we-do/tony-blankley-chair/.

39. William Saletan, "Don't Blame Drones," *Slate,* April 24, 2015.

40. Greg Jaffe, "How Obama went from reluctant warrior to drone champion," *Washington Post*, July 1, 2016, https://www.washingtonpost.com/politics/how-obama-went-from-reluctant-warrior-to-drone-champion/2016/07/01/a41dbd3a-3d53–11e6-a66f-aa6c1883b6b1_story.html.

41. Marcy Wheeler, "Key Area of Dispute on Drone Numbers: Number of Strikes," Empty-Wheel.net, July 13, 2016, http://www.commondreams.org/views/2016/07/13/key-area-dispute-drone-numbers-number-strikes.

42. Ryan Devereaux, "Obama Administration Finally Releases Its Dubious Drone Death Toll," *The Intercept*, July 1, 2016, https://theintercept.com/2016/07/01/obama-administration-finally-releases-its-dubious-drone-death-toll/.

43. John Abizaid and R. Brooks, "Recommendations and Report of the Task Force on Drone Policy." Stimson Center, June 24, 2014, http://www.stimson.org/content/recommendations-and-report-stimson-task-force-us-drone-policy-0.

44. Andrea Shalal, "U.S. needs longer-range, stealthy drones: think tank," Reuters, September 30, 2015, http://www.reuters.com/article/2014/12/10/us-usa-military-technology-idUSKBN0JO08020141210.

45. Lance Menthe, M. Hura, and C. Rhodes, "The Effectiveness of Remotely Piloted Aircraft" (Washington, DC: RAND Corporation, 2014), http://www.rand.org/content/dam/rand/pubs/research_reports/RR200/RR276/RAND_RR276.pdf.

46. Karl Mueller et al., *First Strike: Preemptive and Preventative Attack in US National Strategic Policy* (Santa Monica, CA: RAND Corporation, 2006), 13, http://www.rand.org/content/dam/rand/pubs/monographs/2006/RAND_MG403.pdf.

47. Development, Concepts and Doctrine Centre, *Global Strategic Trends-Out to 2045*, 94–98, https://www.gov.uk/government/uploads/system/uploads/attachment_data/file/348164/20140821_DCDC_GST_5_Web_Secured.pdf.

Chapter Seven

In the News

After having discussed the forces that create information to suit the powerful and the wealthy, it is time to turn to the transmission belt for this information—the news media. Over at least the last fifteen years, the US mainstream news media has repeatedly failed to provide its readers, listeners, and watchers the diversity of information they need in order to make sound conclusions as citizens in a liberal democracy. As far back as the 1980s and 1990s the media largely gave the US government an easy pass when it came to the effectiveness of new high-tech weapons systems, wars of choice such as Grenada and Panama, or support for right-wing dictators and insurgents in Latin America. Even before 2001, as G. William Domhoff has put it:[1]

> The large media play their most important role in the power equation by reinforcing the legitimacy of the social system through the routine ways in which they usually accept and package events. Their style and tone generally take the statements of business and government leaders seriously, treating any claims they make with great respect. This respectful approach is especially noticeable and important in the area of foreign policy, which the media cover in such a way that America's diplomatic aims usually seem honorable and corporate and government involvement overseas is portrayed as necessary and legitimate.

But for at least six years starting with 9/11, they raised the patriotic cheerleading to another level. It led not to a break with the past, but rather to a deepening of existing trends. The Bush administration was able to respond to the 9/11 attacks in the most muddled fashion, virtually without challenge and, in fact, with a good deal of media encouragement. There was almost no mainstream questioning of the breadth of the congressional AUMF, that, fifteen years later, is still used to legitimize US overseas military operations.[2]

Uncovering detainee abuses in Afghanistan, and later Iraq, could hardly be called intrepid as mainstream coverage was forced by the alternative media's original reporting.

The greatest media crime of the early 2000s was the soft coverage of the Bush administration's claim of weapons of mass destruction in Iraq, as well as the revolving door of other reasons to justify the war. The media could have recognized the importance of accountability and self-reflection, while still maintaining their editorial independence. Instead their coverage perpetuated these problems.

The mainstream media coverage has been so mediocre that it has given continued traction to Chalmers Johnson's concept of *blowback*, the sense that an adversary's action is in response to a US action, except that the initial action is "unknown to the American people."[3] Frequently the media did not report the earlier provocation and is disinclined to remind their audience of it as historical background to the current story. Perhaps they feel to do so would be a sign of unforgivable, unpatriotic bias against the US government, people, and their victimhood.

This chapter's discussion is structured to address various issues: media bias, ownership interests, reliance on official sources, government influence, lack of access for war reporting, the media's event orientation, persistence of unasked questions, lack of historical background, and labeling.

One of the themes of this chapter is that, judging from the coverage of drone warfare, the US media did not learn their lesson from the events of the first half of the 2000s. Problems remain with the use of euphemisms and perverse definition of terms, overreliance on official, governmental sources, and lack of commitment to serious investigative journalism. The aphorism that "governments lie," however often it is proven in practice, still doesn't seem to govern or even inform very much of the journalism profession. Perhaps this is no surprise, not only because of the concentration of media ownership, but also because the owners of the media are corporations with strong conflicts of interest, particularly in the production and export of military hardware. War is profitable for the minority even if it imposes great costs on the majority.

MEDIA RESPONSE TO DRONE WARFARE

As Tara McKelvey says in her 2013 study entitled "Media Coverage of the Drone Program," in 2009 and 2010 the media's attention to drone warfare was rather muted considering that at the time the Obama administration was greatly increasing its use of drone attacks. It was, in fact, making drones a central feature of its "kill not capture" military strategy. McKelvey counted articles in five major US print outlets (the *Christian Science Monitor*, the

New York Times, Time magazine, the *Wall Street Journal* and *The Washington Post*). She found 326 articles in 2009, 435 in 2010, 577 in 2011, and 625 in 2012.[4] McKelvey points out that qualitatively the *New York Times* was the leader from the beginning, but from 2009 to 2011 only a handful of articles appeared on the legal questions raised by drone warfare. *The Wall Street Journal* was the most likely to focus on business opportunities; the other outlets were inclined to focus on the involvement of federal agencies and the experience of this new technology for the military.[5]

With the drone killing of US citizen Anwar al-Awlaki in Yemen in the fall of 2011, and Obama's antiterrorism advisor John Brennan's first public speech on drone warfare in early 2012, there is a change in coverage both quantitatively and qualitatively. More questions are asked. It is increasingly recognized that the Obama administration has been the most aggressive in history in prosecuting leakers. This isn't true, however, when the leaks are approved for political purposes or when the leakers are so prominent as to be above reproach, such as Gen. David Petraeus. Names like John Kiriakou, Chelsea Manning, Edward Snowdon, and Jeffrey Sterling are known to those who follow national security prosecutions, though many others act at the behest of senior administration officials and do so with impunity.

The double standard was on full public display as recently as February 2016, when former CIA director Michael Hayden reproduced in a *New York Times* opinion piece what he said was a transcript of an operator conversation before a successful drone strike during his time in the Bush administration. This was written to promote his forthcoming book. While he admits mistakes will occasionally be made, he wrote that "the targeted killing program has been the most precise and effective application of firepower in the history of armed conflict."[6] Why is he allowed to reproduce this transcript while others might be prosecuted for even admitting that the same strike took place? Jesselyn Radack, herself a whistle-blower and lawyer for Edward Snowden, asked how Hayden can admit that civilians have been killed, in contradiction to what John Brennan said in 2011, and not be pressed to provide real data.[7]

No doubt one of the reasons for increasing media attention starting in 2012 can be attributed to the administration's practice of leaking favorable information to defend the program and build up support for itself. In 2009 the CIA killed Taliban leader Baitullah Mehsud in Pakistan and unnamed CIA officials gave off-the-record interviews with details of the assault.[8] No doubt the killing of al-Awlaki was also too good a story to keep quiet, and even if the media presented the leaked story uncritically, it still generated future questions that put public officials under pressure. And that greater media pressure then led Brennan to acknowledge the program and defend its ethical and legal content. Journalists and editors choose to rely too often on official sources.

CIA drone program attacks in Pakistan provide some insight into the importance of pro-administration leaks as well as media bias. What we know about Mehsud's assassination came from an authorized leak. Journalist Gareth Porter explained in October 2013 that the CIA feared the Obama administration might reduce or end the CIA drone campaign in Pakistan. They leaked information to a sympathetic *Post* reporter, Bob Woodward, to the effect that there was a secret agreement between the United States and Pakistan assuring that Pakistan supported the US drone war secretly even if it protested it publicly for domestic consumption. However, as Porter notes, through 2008 Pakistan did appear to support the drone campaign, because attacks were few in number and targeted adversaries of the state, specifically al-Qaeda leaders in Pakistan. However, under the Obama administration in 2009 the United States greatly expanded drone strikes in Pakistan and elsewhere, and broadened the list of those subject to attack. So the United States was making both "signature" and "personality" strikes against members of the Taliban in Pakistan with whom Pakistan had made peace. Yet this is not reported in the story, so that readers are allowed to believe that Pakistani objections are wholly insincere, which greatly undermines sovereignty and international law concerns.[9] The CIA leak in this case also suggests that leaks may be undertaken by one government agency to pursue its own interest even if this is done to undermine or apply pressure on its own side. Contemporary discussions of drone warfare in Pakistan in the mainstream press neglect much of this background, although it is foremost in the minds of its citizens and policy makers.

Sometimes in the interest of the administration, officials oscillate between openness when it works for them and being closed when it doesn't. McKelvey notes that Bush administration officials allowed media tours of the main stateside drone base at Creech AFB, Nevada, until 2009, when access was cut off. Obama officials thought that a journalist had "gone too far" in revealing information about the drone program.[10] However, on May 10, 2009, the CBS flagship current-affairs program *60 Minutes* broadcast a thirteen-minute segment called America's New Air Force. It illustrates all the problems with how the mainstream media has approached the topic, including the fact that journalists often only report what they are told. And they are presented with only positive material. As journalist Lara Logan says in her segment, *60 Minutes* was given extraordinary access to Ground Control units at Creech (the trailers), shots of drone consoles, interviews with drone squadron commanders, visuals of Reapers and Predators, and specially declassified visuals of bad guys getting blown up in Afghanistan and Iraq. We are shown visuals of "a truck full of insurgents being tracked," in which senior stateside commanders can issue an order to fire. There are other cases in which individuals are running away having just attacked US forces, or are carrying a gun, that's hot from being recently fired, according to a drone infrared camera. All are successfully killed. One of the senior officers also says that US ground forces want these eyes in the sky, and that pilots are as engaged as those who are in cockpits. He says drone pilots can concentrate more on their tasks because they do not have the distractions of the physical challenges of flying. This also keeps the enemy (and perhaps everyone else) off balance because it does not know when the USAF is watching.[11]

There is nothing to counterbalance all this happy talk. There is no acknowledgment that at this same time, the CIA was directing drones in Pakistan, with some controversy there. Nor is there an admission that mistakes are made and innocent civilians are killed. There is no recognition that what we now know to be signature strikes may be made on suspicious people, rather than those who have clearly been, or will be, engaged in combat. There is no discussion of the way in which this technology is likely to facilitate permanent war, and certainly no questions about why the United States is still fighting in these countries and elsewhere. The mainstream media has shown little interest in drone program whistle-blowers, such as Brandon Bryant, Michael Haas, Stephen Lewis, and Cian Westmoreland, whose commentary on their own experience as drone warriors for the US Defense Department and the CIA is in line with the argument of this book.[12] *Rolling Stone* magazine, *Democracy Now!* and similar outlets are about the only place you'll see mention of them.

By 2013, the PBS program *Nova* devoted a one-hour episode to this subject matter, called *Rise of the Drones*. Much of the episode focuses on the technological marvel of drone technology for both military and civilian purposes, perhaps not surprising for a program about science and technology. Diversity of opinion comes from an interview with Senator Rand Paul over his concerns with the expected violations of Americans' domestic privacy. It also shows Medea Benjamin of Code Pink disrupting a speech by John Brennan on the grounds of international law and ethics. There is no opportunity for an articulate critique from her, or anyone else, and the episode quotes defense expert Peter W. Singer saying that the United States is fighting the equivalent of an air war in Pakistan without calling it an air war. The program raises the possibility that this is radicalizing people in countries subject to attack. There is also recognition that the drone and operator can lose the satellite link and, with it, control, and that drones can be vulnerable to attack because they are slow and fragile. The producers were given access to drone training at Holloman Air Force Base in New Mexico. Their message is to fixate on the technology and to accept that it allows the USAF to kill the right people while avoiding killing civilians. One of the two major named funders of the series was the David H. Koch Fund for Science, which provides an indication of conservative support for the program, and possibly a conservative influence.[13]

CHOICE OF WORDS

As noted earlier, use of the phrase *targeted killing* is favored by the US government because killing is something that legitimately happens in war (unlike assassination and murder). *Targeted* means that the US military knows who it is killing. Another renamed term is *militant*. Historically a militant was an individual who carried arms, usually in an insurgency or revolution, while a uniformed member of contemporary, state-based militaries was called a soldier. But as Glenn Greenwald points out, reflecting on a *New York Times* article, as of May 2012 the Obama administration had redefined *militant* to mean "military-age males in a strike zone," unless after the fact the individual is proven to be a noncombatant. The administration's rationale is that jihadi terrorists only consort with other jihadi terrorists, and therefore any male of military age can be assumed to be a participant in the movement.[14]

Those who know anything about Middle Eastern societies know that where extended families and tribal connections are important, genuine militants do regularly interact with nonmilitants just by virtue of going about their daily lives. Further, out of one side of its mouth the administration criticizes militants for living among innocents, and out of the other side it claims it can kill militants without killing innocents, even with so-called signature strikes! Greenwald's problem is that whenever the media repeat administration claims about several "militants killed," they are "knowingly disseminating a false and misleading term of propaganda." Maybe only genuine militants were killed, but it is equally or more likely in some cases that male civilians were also killed.

This situation is aggravated by the innovation of referring to "personality" and signature strikes. Personality strikes are those drone or other strikes in which a known person is targeted, someone like al-Awlaki or other identifiable individual who is on the kill list. In this situation civilians can be killed, either with or without US admission. However, the Obama administration also makes reference to signature strikes that are attacks on groups of individuals, who exhibit "suspicious behavior" or who fit the profile of terrorists or other militants. The reality is that the United States doesn't really know who it's killing, and given the state of the bodies after the attack there may be no way of conclusively finding out. A personality or signature strike is often reported without discussion of what this means.

THE WORTH OF A PICTURE

It is well known that the US government does not routinely release footage of aerial attacks (and not even footage of returning coffins of US military personnel), so that most images come from leakers such as Chelsea Manning and others. There are often no graphics in television media coverage or there are unrealistic ones. Scholars in communications and psychology have done experiments to test reactions and see what, if any, effects come from realistic versus substituted images in media reporting. Erica Scharrer and Greg Blackburn conducted a study in which they showed viewers media coverage of drone strikes and other topics and then surveyed them on their reactions. They found that viewers had greater empathy for the victims of drone strikes when they saw more graphic images. The researchers concluded that they were not desensitized by them. The viewers were not necessarily more negative toward US policy on the use of drones,[15] though this could also be because that last assessment is based on many factors including citizens' general calculations of the cost of benefits of drone warfare for the United States, particularly in the short term.

Cameron Riopelle and Parthiban Muniandy point to the (inaccurate) messages that graphics convey on *CBS World News* online. In an academic article they reproduced sixteen images from *CBS World News* online graphics and argue that there is a decontextualization of maps, a recycling of the same graphics for very different stories, a conflation of Islam and the Middle East as one and the same, and a monolithic representation of Islam. These patterns will be familiar to those who watch network television. In some graphics, omnipotent Reaper or Predator drones, or cruise missiles, loom large over maps of particular countries like Libya, Pakistan, and Yemen. Other graphics show Islamic symbols, shadowy figures sometimes carrying weapons, or unflattering photos of adversarial leaders such as Moammar Qaddafi. In the last case, the graphic that announces the death of Qaddafi shows silhouettes of jubilant figures, a clear indication of the intention to convey political content.[16]

DELIVERING THE RIGHT MESSAGE

The media also almost universally present the idea that drone warfare is popular within the United States. The Obama administration is positive about drones, and it should be no surprise that it would want to minimize public opposition and maximize public support. One way is to maintain secrecy for as long as possible. American people don't know that there are one hundred drone missions per day and that, frankly, there is every reason to believe that this will be a permanent condition. Another way is to discourage mainstream discussion of issues that are being raised in this book and other works. Finally, the administration would benefit if polling showed that drones are popular, to reassure policy makers and elected officials that this major change will not have any negative political fallout.

In September 2015 Glenn Greenwald pointed out that reporting in the *New York Times* provided false information on the US attitude towards cluster bombs. Rick Gladstone of the *Times* had written a story on the Cluster Munitions Coalition's critique of the five states that used cluster bombs in 2015—Libya, Sudan, Syria, Ukraine, and Yemen. He wrote that "the use of these weapons was criticized by all 117 countries that have joined the treaty, which took effect five years ago. Their use was also criticized by a number of others, including the United States, that have not yet joined the treaty but have abided by its provisions." It is hard to believe that the United States really opposed the use of cluster bombs because the country is one of the world's leading producers. Cluster bombs are particularly controversial because they are largely an anticivilian weapon causing many bomblets to be released and scattered over large areas. Further, a small percentage of bomblets are duds and, like antipersonnel mines, they can lie in wait and explode at a future time, including when they are handled by children. As Greenwald says, the United States could not abide by the treaty, because to do so would be to stop producing, stockpiling, and exporting cluster bombs.[17] Mainstream media are still providing their consumers with reassurance that the United States is doing its part to create a more orderly world.

Are we really sure, however, that drones are so popular? As Sarah Kreps has pointed out, the actual degree of citizen support for drone warfare depends on the questions pollsters ask. She notes that many criticisms have been made, but that "these criticisms have tended not to translate into lower levels of support for drones strikes because contemporary polling has restricted the frame of reference for how individuals evaluate the policy." As she says, the polling questions often look something like this: "Do you favor or oppose the use of unmanned aircraft, also known as drones, to kill suspected members of al-Qaeda and other terrorists?" Or, perhaps, do you approve of using drones to "launch airstrikes in other countries against suspected terrorists?" It is generally accepted that, particularly in 2011 through 2013, strong majorities answered that they approved.

In response, Kreps developed an experimental design asking individuals for their level of support. Questions were modified to account for International Humanitarian Law concerns about lack of distinction regarding noncombatants, lack of proportionality, legal concerns about absence of domestic US authorization, and nonconformity with international law. Kreps found that majority support suddenly becomes minority support when these doubts are raised.[18] This shows how public opinion is constructed and reconstructed, and not that it has preexisting stable and unchanging existence. More information will change how people answer the survey, and in a liberal democratic society those results can be used either to bolster those who advocate or oppose drone warfare. It is worth mentioning that pollsters are not asking questions about citizens' support for drone warfare based on an acceptance that other countries, including potential adversaries, either now have or will soon have weaponized drone capacity as well. Clearly, the media play a key role.

CONCLUSION

As this chapter suggests, the treatment of drone warfare in the mainstream US media has reproduced the disastrous problems of the 2000s when reporters and columnists rarely questioned decisions made by the Bush administration. Because of this, the media must take some responsibility for the unnecessary invasion of Iraq and the calamity that followed. The media are mostly timid in challenging the interests of corporate ownership and continue to rely on official sources. The US government treats the most sympathetic media in a special way, assuring that its message is presented in a complimentary fashion. This form of journalism leaves many unasked questions and incomplete historical context. Drone warfare may be less popular than the media imply, given that people are reacting to a sanitized version with no awareness of possible long-term results. Does the American public truly understand drone warfare? Do Americans have any idea of the concept of permanent war? Because drone warfare has not taken many direct American lives, the story has not been adequately presented. The media has a lot of work to do to ensure that the public has the facts and the analysis to move forward.

NOTES

1. G. William Domhoff, *Who Rules America?* 126.
2. This is also not the first time that the United States has gotten into difficulty with overly broad authorizations, exemplified by the UN Security Council Resolution on Korea in June 1950 and the Congressional Gulf of Tonkin Resolution in 1965.
3. Chalmers Johnson, *Blowback: The Costs and Consequences of American Empire*, 2nd ed. (New York: Holt Paperbacks, 2004).
4. Tara McKelvey, "Media Coverage of the Drone Program," Joan Shorenstein Center on the Press, Politics and Public Policy, Harvard University, Discussion Paper D-77 (February 2013), 21.
5. Ibid., 4–5.
6. Michael Hayden, "To Keep America Safe, Embrace Drone Warfare," *New York Times*, February 19, 2016, http://www.nytimes.com/2016/02/21/opinion/sunday/drone-warfare-precise-effective-imperfect.html?_r=1.
7. Vegas Tenold, "Badass Attorney Shoots Down the Case for Drones," *Rolling Stone*, February 24, 2016, http://www.rollingstone.com/politics/news/badass-attorney-shoots-down-the-case-for-drones-20160224.
8. McKelvey, "Media Coverage," 14. See note 4 above.
9. Gareth Porter, "US: *Washington Post* Drone Story Ignored PAK Military Opposition to Strikes," *Global Information Network*, October 25, 2013.
10. McKelvey, "Media Coverage," 12.
11. Lara Logan, "America's New Air Force." *60 Minutes*, May 10, 2019.

12. Tenold, "The Untold Casualties of the Drone War," *Rolling Stone*, February 18, 2016, http://www.rollingstone.com/politics/news/the-untold-casualties-of-the-drone-war-20160218.

13. Peter Yost, "Rise of the Drones," *Nova*, January 23, 2013.

14. Glenn Greenwald, "'Militants': media propaganda," *Salon*, May 29, 2012, http://www.salon.com/2012/05/29/militants_media_propaganda/.

15. Erica Sharrer and Greg Blackburn, "Images of Injury: Graphic News Visuals' Effects," *Mass Communication and Society*, May 2015.

16. Cameron Riopelle and Parthiban Muniandy, "Drones, maps and crescents," *Media, War and Conflict* 6(2): 153–72.

17. Greenwald, "NYT Claims U.S. Abides by Cluster Bomb Treaty," *The Intercept*, September 3, 2015, https://theintercept.com/2015/09/03/nyt-claims-u-s-abides-cluster-bomb-ban-exact-opposite-reality/.

18. Sarah Kreps, "Flying under the radar," *Research and Politics* April-June 2014: 1–7.

Chapter Eight

Sites of Resistance

International Law and Social Movements

Drone weapons make it much easier to intervene militarily in countries with which one is not legally or formally at war. The deploying power can intervene very selectively in states more overtly than small-scale "cloak-and-dagger" missions but without leaving its fingerprints in a way that the use of conventional infantry, helicopters, or fighter-bombers do.

Drone attacks are also easier to keep secret from your domestic population than other forms of intervention, with the exception of small-scale, covert operations using conventional military forces. This means that the state that possesses weaponized drone aircraft can undertake military operations in more countries at far lower cost, with lower domestic political fallout. For the United States, this is a formula for increased overseas military operations in countries where there has been no explicit congressional authorization or declaration of war, such as Yemen and Pakistan. Sarah Kreps has commented that the increasing availability of drones might introduce "moral hazard," because of those "situations whereby avoiding costs has the perverse incentive of causing one actor to engage in risks that they would not otherwise take."[1] Yet, as we have also seen, the history of military competition and conflict since the 1860s has been one of initial enthusiasm for technological breakthroughs followed by the disappointment that comes from the widespread dissemination of the same weapons. The development of the repeating rifle, the machine gun, the tank, mustard and chlorine gas, the submarine, the rocket, the atomic bomb, and so on, enabled the first to have them to gain a temporary advantage, only to see themselves checked as others developed similar weapons.

Scholars of international relations and foreign policy have oscillated between enthusiasm for the monopoly over a new weapon, and realization that peace will only be kept by deterrence (or by limits placed by treaties) once the weapons are acquired by numerous parties.[2] It may not yet be obvious to the general public, but citizens are resisting drone warfare in various ways, including legal debates over their use, the use of law to defend those who commit civil disobedience, and international treaties to limit drone use. The success of the international coalition to ban antipersonnel landmines is a useful model to follow. This chapter presents these attempts to resist drone warfare through international law and social movements.

US AND GLOBAL APPROACHES TO THE INTERNATIONAL LAW OF WAR

Since 2001 it has appeared that US experts in international law are much more likely to support their country's actions in the world than are international lawyers from elsewhere. US media have an easier time finding US-based international legal scholars who support the Bush/Obama policy, which then gives observers the impression that the international law community accepts administration claims. This is particularly true in the case of assassination and extrajudicial execution. Non-US scholars are more skeptical of US government doctrine, whether it is the question of detention of prisoners, or the use of assassination as a technique through on-the-ground hit teams or drone aircraft.[3]

Kenneth Anderson, for example, sees "stand-off targeted killing" as appropriate, based on the idea that this is part of the right to self-defense "short of armed conflict."[4] For some, a defense of Israeli assassination, which predated similar US activities by several years, provides justification by extension. Nicholas Kendall, for example, defends Israeli assassinations in the West Bank and Gaza, claiming that they are a response to attacks from "foreign territory" and part of "anticipatory self-defense."[5] However, these scholars are often inconsistent in how the West Bank and Gaza are considered. For some purposes they will claim that these two zones have no sovereign power at all, reminiscent of the Spanish and Christian European view of the New World, which was said to have no sovereignty because there were no Christian princes. These territories are recognized as Occupied Territories for which Israel has responsibility; the preferred global solution is some form of independent self-government exercised by their residents.

Michael Gross asks why liberal democracies engage in assassination, torture, and blackmail. His response is an astute one, for he notes that because of asymmetry, the great inequality between the Western countries (especially the United States and United Kingdom) and the rest of the world, there has been no reciprocal violent response to these activities.[6] Andrew Altman and Christopher Heath Wellman claim that if armed intervention can sometimes be justified, then so too can assassination of leaders, since this is the less "risky" action.[7] Daniel Statman claims that assassination is an acceptable substitute because conventional war does not work.[8] Robert Chesney argues that it is acceptable for the United States to target American citizen Anwar al-Awlaki, without addressing the degree to which this is a violation of US law, even if it is done outside the country.[9]

Often these arguments are weakened by the authors' tendency to look at issues in isolation without considering the larger context. For example, those who say that a certain kind of attack or assassination is acceptable simply assume that the *jus ad bellum* issue, the legitimacy of the war in the first place, is resolved in the affirmative. If initiation of the war was a large crime (clearly the case in Iraq, an act of aggression by the United States and its Coalition of the Willing), then shouldn't the aggressors leave the country and negotiate the payment of reparations, rather than rationalize combat techniques that will only prolong the situation or make it worse? Realist scholars of international law, those who ultimately see power politics at the base of everything, have been known to say that the system of international law really codifies a past or aging system of global relations. From the perspective of this "might-makes-right" school, it is natural that a unipolar world requires a new system of international law, one that allows latitude to the hegemonic power (i.e., the United States). It should be no surprise that this pro-US international law commentary often claims that the old rules are vague, and not really as restrictive as they seem.[10]

This debate is also being felt outside the United States. In the United Kingdom, a Joint Parliamentary Committee on Human Rights issued a report in May 2016 cautioning the British government on the legal jeopardy that political leaders and military officers may be put in because of the expanded use of weaponized drones in countries that the United Kingdom is not at war with. The British government has killed both British and non-British citizens in drone strikes outside Iraq and Afghanistan. As journalists Alice Ross and Owen Bowcott write: "'We owe it to all those involved in the chain of command for such uses of lethal force to provide them with absolute clarity about the circumstances in which they will have a defense against any possible future criminal prosecution, including those which might originate from outside the UK', says the committee, chaired by the former Labour deputy leader Harriet Harman, MP." The committee suggested that while the British government is unlikely to prosecute Britons for their participation in drone warfare, prosecution services in other countries might look at it differently, particularly where their own nationals have been killed.[11] It is also worth mentioning that the United Kingdom, unlike the United States, has ratified the Rome Statute and its citizens are subject to the jurisdiction of the International Criminal Court headquartered in The Hague.

RESISTING DRONE NATION

Citizens are resisting the rise of "Drone Nation" through direct action or more creative means. People of conscience have been protesting and, in some cases, engaging in civil disobedience at drone air force bases. John Dear, S.J., provides an account of his trial in Nevada, with thirteen codefendants, for "criminal trespassing" during their protest at Creech Air Force Base, April 9, 2009. For the defendants, it was victory enough to have the judge hear arguments about international law, the necessity defense, and drone warfare from expert witnesses such as former US attorney general Ramsey Clark, Col. Ann Wright (US Army, Ret.) and Bill Quigley from the Centre for Constitutional Rights.[12] Some years later, a fifty-eight-year-old grandmother of three, Mary Anne Grady-Flores, was sentenced to a year in county jail for repeatedly protesting drones at New York Air National Guard Hancock field.[13] Visual artists are also reflecting on "Drone Nation," as in a 2012 exhibition in Munich. They point out the startling uniformity of images in material distributed on drones and drone warfare, while below the surface most people don't really know much about what's going on, despite seeming media saturation.[14]

Once the public loses its enthusiasm for drone warfare, once drone warfare is no longer considered cool in popular culture, what steps can be taken to prohibit or limit it? One answer is found in the treaty power in international law. Some say that international law is toothless and not worth pursuing. They note that great powers in particular are able to invade other countries and violate sovereignty seemingly with impunity. But most international law is followed most of the time, and while it is not the only way to address weaponized drones, it is one valuable path to pursue.

Since the last half of the nineteenth century in particular, the global community has been discontent with a *laissez-faire* attitude when it comes to the outbreak and conduct of warfare. Since the 1890s, activists have tried to use the treaty mechanism both to reduce the outbreak of warfare and to eliminate the harshest tactics. The widespread ratification of the UN Charter was aimed at greatly reducing the likelihood of war, with the five permanent members of the Security Council acting in concert. Before that, there were efforts to control the size and number of naval ships, to control other forms of war, and to ban war altogether. One of the early treaties was the St. Petersburg Declaration of 1868, designed to ban explosive or incendiary bullets; the Geneva Gas Protocol of 1925 finally prohibited the use of poisonous gases in war, after the terrible experience of World War I. Since World War II, there has been greater success in treaty writing. The use of chemical and biological weapons has largely been banned, and there have been considerable efforts to create treaties to prevent the proliferation of nuclear weapons and other weapons of mass destruction.

Treaties and protocols also exist that restrict or ban conventional weapons, including the intentional use of white phosphorus, cluster bombs, and, most successfully, antipersonnel land mines. Most people would agree that a global ban on atomic weapons in the mid-1940s, after the United States used the bomb in Japan and before the Soviet Union and China developed it, would have been a great achievement. There were discussions at the time, but the lack of trust prevented an agreement.

Notwithstanding the small Israeli arsenal, the United States has a virtual monopoly on weaponized drones, though this won't be true by 2020. Part of the purpose of this work is to discuss the current US love affair with drone warfare, but also to show the medium- to long-term consequences of this infatuation. US policy makers and citizens may not realize this, or may be in denial, but the United States is generating a great deal of hostility because of its drone attacks. It is creating a situation (a "security dilemma" in the words of experts) in which the logical course of action for friend and foe alike is to embark on a new arms race. All sides can then acquire both the capacity to identify and destroy drones, as well as to develop a fleet of weaponized drones. We are not far from the day in which victims of drone attacks may have the capacity to destroy *most* of these aircraft before they reach their target areas, while they also develop the capacity to fly their own drone missions over the airspace of Boston, New York, Los Angeles, and Washington, DC.

The next move for the global community is to push for limits on the use of drone aircraft, precisely because they tend to widen warfare to a global level and reinforce the Augustinian idea of war –the targeting of, and revenge against, specific leaders and individuals. In their introduction to a major edited collection about land mines, M. A. Cameron, R. J. Lawson, and B. W. Tomlin note that by the 1980s and 1990s humanitarians were aware of the particularly egregious legacy of antipersonnel land mines. These land mines were laid in dozens of countries in the 1950s through 1980s by military forces to protect their encampments or to cover their movements or retreats. At three to five dollars per unit, these mines would not usually be removed by the party that laid them. They would explode, maim, and kill civilians years, and even decades, later. These explosives were produced by many countries and were standard issue as the United States and Soviet Union provided military support in the proxy wars during the Cold War, in many countries in the global South. The weapons were classic candidates for limitation or elimination by treaty. Of dubious military value, in the medium- to long-term they were more likely to injure noncombatants, in opposition to the rules of war, than to injure combatants during conflict.[15]

SETTING A GOOD EXAMPLE: THE VICTORY OVER LANDMINES

The International Campaign to Ban Landmines, launched in 1992, is a "global civil-society" coalition of more than one thousand nongovernmental organizations (NGOs) devoted to the relief of those injured by exploding land mines, and the elimination of landmines as a tool of war. The campaign forged links and cooperated with a number of middle powers including Canada and Norway. The more that people around the world learned about the reality of the land mines legacy, the more horrified they became. Suddenly there was political support to do something about it. The "Ottawa Process," as it was called, began in October 1996, and fourteen months later, in December 1997, the treaty was finalized. Ratified by a sufficient number of states in record time, it makes the production, transfer, and possession of large numbers of antipersonnel (AP) mines illegal. Signatory states have committed to destroy their stockpiles and to provide aid to states that have the task of de-mining parts of their territory.[16]

The experience of the Ottawa Process is pertinent in our ongoing challenge to eliminate and control conventional weapons, including weaponized drones. First, this process showed the importance of a large civil-society movement in favor of reducing and eliminating AP mines. Second, because this was a treaty among states, NGOs found that state allies were of fundamental importance. Middle powers have resources unavailable to the NGO sector and can get issues on the global agenda. Even a small state can make a significant impact when it can concentrate its diplomatic and financial resources. These states were able to defy one or more of the great powers, which predictably opposed the effort. This is a strong concrete example of the exercise of "soft power" that comes from diplomatic efforts rather than the "hard power" from money and military resources. It also speaks to the importance of the small- and medium-sized states working together. As Shannon Smith commented, the Ottawa Process was successful because activists decided to surround "the cities with the villages: isolated, the cities will fall."[17] If cities hold out against global opinion, it undermines their claim of leadership and enlightenment.

Third, as Stephen Goose and Nobel laureate Jody Williams note, the mine ban treaty was successful because a large majority of participants abandoned the "consensus model," in which an agreement that means little but enjoys virtually universal support is reached, but is by definition ineffective.[18] Rather, participants accepted that a small number of great powers would inevitably oppose the initiative but they wouldn't allow them to derail the achievement. Fourth, the treaty has been successful because the NGOs did not disband or move on once the treaty was signed. They persisted to ensure that state commitments to ratify it were met. NGOs have also played an important role in overseeing the implementation of the treaty and keeping the issue in the global public eye. Interestingly, Williams, a major force in the land mine ban process, has herself moved on to drones and has called for a ban.

CRUCIAL NEW EFFORTS

There are important rumblings in civil society about taking steps to control "Drone Nation," including in the United States, where arguments come through in congressional resistance to current drone policy. For example, the "International Committee for Robot Arms Control" (ICRAC) is an organization that is devoted to pushing for the application of conventional arms control to the drone sector. Beyond the problems of the proliferation of these weapons, and the fact that they lend themselves to violations of the international law of war, there are some central issues in the not-too-distant future that should be addressed now. It is only a matter of time before weapons of mass destruction are loaded onto drones, which makes them, as first-strike weapons, as or more destabilizing than quick-strike cruise missiles. The challenge of these drones will be felt particularly by those states in Central and East Asia that find themselves ringed by US military bases, including drone bases. The People's Republic of China, Pakistan, and India do not have a reciprocal capacity to launch drone strikes on US territory. The other challenge, perhaps not far in the future, is current research that takes the human out of the equation and make drones fully autonomous, including on the decision to fire.

There are now public glimpses of research on topics such as computer recognition of human gestures and body language, including the meaning of raised hands as a "surrender" sign, leading, hopefully, to a "do not fire" decision. Ronald Arkin, of the Mobile Robot Laboratory in the College of Computing at Georgia Tech, has produced a lengthy technical report, funded by the US Army Research Office, on how to embed ethics in "robot architecture." His goal is to write software to incorporate the laws of war and rules of engagement to allow robots to self-govern. He says: "It is not my belief that an unmanned system will be able to be perfectly ethical in the battlefield, but I am convinced that they can perform more ethically than human soldiers are capable of." Citing a 2006 report of the Mental Health Advisory Team IV (Office of the US Surgeon General), Arkin points out that US soldiers and marines in Iraq were distressingly inclined to mistreat combatants and noncombatants alike, to countenance torture, and to cover up for fellow soldiers who needlessly harmed Iraqi civilians. He asserts that autonomous robotic systems will be able to do better than this,[19] though he does not entertain the idea that the US military should not be in these countries in the first place. While he does not go as far as Williams and others, he has called for a moratorium on the use of robotic weapons to ensure that they are used properly and with the necessary safeguards.[20]

Where Arkin might be labeled a techno-optimist, Noel Sharkey, a robotics and artificial intelligence professor at the United Kingdom's University of Sheffield, and a cofounder of ICRAC, is more pessimistic. Sharkey argues that we are not even close to being able to substitute machine judgment for human judgments. He points out that the use of military force, particularly in counterinsurgency, requires highly refined and experienced assessments of the difference between civilians and combatants. Techniques that might work in the lab, such as scanning facial expressions, won't work when subjects are moving or when their faces are obscured or covered. He suggests that the greatest risk is just what Arkin and others are working on—the fully autonomous, weaponized drone—in part because no person can be held responsible. Responsibility is the key to the laws of war. "There is no way to punish a robot. We could just switch it off but it would not care anymore about that than my washing machine would care. Imagine telling your washing machine that if it does not remove stains properly you will break its door off. Would you expect that to have any impact?"[21]

One might add that the other problem of autonomous drones is that by definition they are "unlawful combatants." As US captives in Afghanistan have heard many times, to be a lawful combatant you must be an individual in the conventional military, or, as provided by Article 4(A) (2) (a) of the Third Geneva Convention, you must be "commanded by a person responsible for his subordinates" among other things. Autonomous drones don't qualify on any basis.

But what makes weaponized drones so dangerous that they should be the subject of "preventative arms control?" Relative to other weapons and tactics, such as the violent confrontation of two armies, drone warfare represents a serious threat to humanity's thoroughly articulated rules on the conduct of warfare. These rules are not there to be swept aside by a newly dominant power, as the US government increasingly would have us do. They are one of the great achievements of the twentieth century and, in fact, must be used to restrain twenty-first century states.

Drawing from I. J. MacLeod and A. P. V. Rogers, an examination of the development of arms control treaties since the mid-1860s allows us to identify four general principles that can be considered part of customary international law. These are: 1) that weapons should not cause unnecessary suffering or superfluous injury; 2) that weapons must not be indiscriminate in their effects; 3) that weapons must not be treacherous in their nature; and 4) that weapons must not be abhorrent to ordinary people.[22] As we have seen, drone aircraft do cause unnecessary and superfluous injury in part because the operator is possibly many thousands of miles away. Killing is sanitized and information is more limited than a situation in which soldiers with a translator are questioning individuals on the ground or apprehending someone on the most-wanted list. The only way that drone attacks do not kill civilians is if the victims are defined as combatants or militants after they are killed, as the United States has tried to do.

Drones are also treacherous because they attack targets without any regard for theaters of war or traditional rules of engagement. In international humanitarian law, treachery is defined as perfidy, specifically the use of deception to instill in your adversary confidence that he or she is entitled to receive privileged status, or that the adversary must confer privileged status and that no harm will be done. More concretely, this takes the form of feigning a truce or surrender, feigning incapacitation by wounds or sickness, feigning noncombatant or protected status, or using undercover personnel to do the fighting that is appropriately done by those in uniform.[23] Drone aerial attacks are the equivalent of undercover operations because they abandon the distinction between the battlefield and the rear and they do not provide transparency as to who has made the attack. So when a Hellfire missile comes out of the sky without warning, possibly in a country where no state of war exists, and kills individuals who are not bearing arms and may even be "out of combat" (*hors de combat*), or never have borne arms, this is a form of treachery and a violation of international law.

Finally, these weapons are likely to be abhorrent to ordinary people as they learn more about them, just as they found abhorrent AP landmines, cluster bombs, and the targeting of people with white phosphorus. The international medical organization Medact also argues that drone warfare should be included in treaty negotiations and banned because it inflicts continuous psychological injuries on subject populations, including those who are never targeted.[24]

Beyond garnering inspiration from the AP mine ban treaty, there are certainly international law instruments that could be amended to regulate the use of weaponized drones. A leading example among international treaties is actually called the Convention on Prohibitions or Restrictions on the Use of Certain Conventional Weapons which may be deemed to be Excessively Injurious or to have Indiscriminate Effects. It came into force on December 2, 1983, based on state ratifications largely from what was then called the Soviet bloc as well as other state-socialist countries, including China, Laos, Yugoslavia, and a few others in Europe. The convention, and particularly the three protocols, do ban certain weapons, including those that injure by fragments not detectable by X-rays (Protocol I). It also restricts the use of mines and booby-traps (Protocol II) and certain incendiary weapons (Protocol III). The convention is not well known and has had little effect, in part because it was produced by the consensus model of diplomacy, catering in its language to those who would not sign or ratify the convention in any event. It is no exaggeration to say that it is full of "weasel words." For example, Protocol III might well be interpreted to ban the use of white phosphorus, which has been used by the United States in Iraq and by Israel in Gaza. But it only bans incendiary weapons that are defined as *"primarily designed* to set fire to objects or to cause burn injury to persons . . ." (emphasis added).[25] Current users of white phosphorus claim that its *primary design purpose* is to illuminate the battlefield; they say that damage to people or property is an unintended consequence, and therefore the use is legal.

Issues such as opposition to the weaponization of drones, the killing of both US citizens and foreign civilians, and general concerns about drones as a means to eliminate individual privacy, are finding their way onto the agenda of all three levels of US government. For example, writer David Swanson has drafted a resolution for his home city's council, Charlottesville, Virginia, that calls for a ban on US extrajudicial killing, the use of drones for surveillance, and the weaponization of drones within the United States. It declares that Charlottesville is to become a drone-free jurisdiction with the exception of the activities of hobbyists under certain controlled conditions.[26] There have also been some efforts to bring in a ban of drone warfare activities in the European Union.[27] The pressure against drone warfare is significant as major European powers decide whether to develop drone fleets, whether drones will be a major military export product line, and whether they will continue to cooperate with current US efforts, as the United Kingdom and Germany are doing.[28]

People are aware of Senator Rand Paul's critique of drone warfare and especially domestic use of drones; it is also clear that he became less critical of drones, which has been attributed to his failed run for the 2016 Republican presidential nomination.[29] Yet there are many on the libertarian right who continue to challenge Obama administration drone policy. Republican Rep. Thomas Massie, also of Kentucky, introduced the "Life, Liberty, and Justice for All Americans Act" in March 2013. Massie and his cosponsors propose that Congress prevent "the executive branch from authorizing military strikes upon American citizens on American soil."[30] There has been no clear answer from the Obama administration as to whether the US government can kill Americans at home, since it can do so overseas. The libertarian right believes it fits into the *posse commitatus* tradition that says that the US military cannot be active in domestic US affairs. They are particularly suspicious when the commander-in-chief is a Democrat.

Retired representative Ron Paul continues to express skepticism of current US drone warfare and foreign and defense policy more generally, through the vehicle of the Ron Paul Institute for Peace and Prosperity. He was particularly exercised over the revelation of the unintended killing of US citizen Dr. Warren Weinstein in Pakistan in early 2015, as well as the less-covered overseas assassination of two US citizens said to have joined al Qaeda.[31] There are others, such as former Bush official Jack Goldsmith, who describes himself as having "gone ACLU" on the question of drone warfare, in light of the expansion of the use of drones in the Obama era.[32] The American Civil Liberties Union promotes strict adherence to the Bill of Rights, often placing the organization at odds with conservatives in the United States.

CONCLUSION

Public anti-drone sentiment may not be loud but it is percolating, even in the United States. Discussion in this chapter focused on ways that can be used to capitalize on it—specifically international laws and treaties. A presentation of problems with assassination in general, and specifically drone warfare, was followed up with how international law and treaty mechanisms should be used to address drone warfare as the new and unlawful frontline of international aggression. The unique, exciting, and successful process resulting in the International Coalition to Ban Landmines sets a strong example and can certainly be pursued regarding drone weapons. Just as there were countries such as Canada and Norway that were willing to take the lead on the AP mine ban, Pakistan, Iraq, and even Afghanistan may be prepared to step forward and speak out on the use of weaponized drones, particularly if and when the US grip is eased in these countries. As the historic anti-landmine battle proved, strong, informed, and organized citizen action creates positive results.

NOTES

1. Sarah Kreps, *Drones* (New York: Oxford University Press, 2016), 48.
2. An interesting discussion of drone warfare in this light is found in J. Altmann, "Preventive Arms Control for Uninhabited Military Vehicles," *Ethics and Robotics* (2009), 69–82.
3. Mary Ellen O'Connell, "Unlawful Killing with Combat Drones: A Case Study of Pakistan, 2004–2009," Notre Dame Law School Legal Studies Research Paper Series 9.43 (2010): 1–26.
4. Kenneth Anderson, "Targeted Killing in U.S. Counterterrorism Strategy and Law," *Legislating the War on Terror: An Agenda for Reform*, Washington, DC: Brookings Institution Press, 2009.
5. J. Nicholas Kendall, "Israeli Counter-Terrorism: 'Targeted Killings' Under International Law," *North Carolina Law Review* 80 (2002): 1069–88.
6. Michael Gross, "Assassination and Targeted Killing: law Enforcement, Execution or Self-Defence?" *Journal of Applied Philosophy* 23(3 [2006]): 323–35.
7. Andrew Altman and Christopher Heath Wellman, "From Humanitarian Intervention to Assassination: Human Rights and Political Violence," *Ethics* 118(2 [2008]): 228–57.

8. Daniel Statman, "Targeted Killing," *Theoretical Inquiries in Law* 5(1 [2004]): 179–98.

9. Robert Chesney, "Who May Be Killed? Anwar al-Awlaki as a Case Study in the International Legal Regulation of Lethal Force," *Yearbook of International Humanitarian Law* 13 (2010): 3–60.

10. See Mark V. Vlasic, "Assassination and Targeted Killing—A Historical and Post-Bin Laden Legal Analysis," *Georgetown Journal of International Law* XXXXIII (2012), 279 ff., for analysis along these lines.

11. Alice Ross and O. Bowcott, "UK drone strikes," *The Guardian*, May 10, 2016, http://www.theguardian.com/politics/2016/may/10/uk-drone-strikes-murder-charges-clarify-legal-basis-targeted-kill-policy-isis.

12. John Dear, S. J., "A peace movement victory in court," *National Catholic Reporter*, September 21, 2010, http://www.fatherjohndear.org/articles/a-peace-movement-victory-in-court.html.

13. Nathan Mattise, "Grandma repeatedly protested drones at base, now faces a year in jail," *Arstechnica*, July 13, 2014, http://arstechnica.com/tech-policy/2014/07/grandma-repeatedly-protested-drones-at-base-now-faces-a-year-in-prison/.

14. Rachel Somerstein, "We can't remember what we haven't seen," *Afterimage* 40(4 [Jan/Feb 2013]): 10–14.

15. This section is drawn from the editors' introduction, "To Walk without Fear," in *To Walk Without Fear: The Global Movement to Ban Landmines* edited by in M. A. Cameron, R. J. Lawson and B. W. Tomlin, 1–19 (Toronto: Oxford University Press, 1998).

16. Ibid., 5–10.

17. Shannon Smith, "Surround the Cities with the Villages: Universalization of the Mine Ban Treaty," in *Banning Landmines: Disarmament, Citizen Diplomacy and Human Security* edited by J. Williams, S. Goose and M. Wareham, 69–86 (Lanham, MD: Rowman and Littlefield Publishers, 2008).

18. Williams and S. Goose, "Citizen Diplomacy and the Ottawa Process: A lasting model?" in *Banning Landmines*, chap. 11.

19. Ronald C. Arkin, "Governing Lethal Behavior: Embedding Ethics in a Hybrid Deliberative/Reactive Robot Architecture," 7–8, http://www.cc.gatech.edu/ai/robot-lab/online-publications/formalizationv35.pdf.

20. Stuart Hughes, "Campaigners call for international ban on 'killer robots,'" BBC, April 23, 2013, http://www.bbc.com/news/uk-22250664.

21. Noel Sharkey, "Weapons of indiscriminate Lethality," *FIfF Kommunikation*, January 2009: 26–28.

22. I. J. MacLeod and A. P. V. Rogers, "The Use of White Phosphorus and the Law of War," *Yearbook of International Humanitarian Law* X (75–97 [2007]), 83.

23. Nils Melzer, *Targeted Killing in International Law* (Oxford: Oxford University Press, 2008), 372–73.

24. Sarah Boseley, "Drones should be included in arms reduction treaties," *The Guardian*, October 13, 2012, http://www.theguardian.com/world/2012/oct/13/drones-arms-reduction-treaties.

25. The English text of the convention is found in the United Nations Treaty Series, Vol. 1342, 1983, 163–72.

26. David Swanson, "A New Model Drone Resolution," *Counterpunch*, January 25, 2013, http://www.counterpunch.org/2013/01/25/a-new-model-drone-resolution/.

27. "Drone strikes to continue," *Russia Today*.

28. European Section, Global Anti-Drone Network, "'Ban Weaponized Drones,'" Truthout, December 19, 2013, http://www.truth-out.org/speakout/item/20740-ban-weaponized-drones-anti-drone-movement-spreads-in-europe.

29. Steve Benen, "Rand Paul's drone 'evolution' now complete," The Maddow Blog, April 27, 2015, http://www.msnbc.com/rachel-maddow-show/rand-pauls-drone-evolution-now-complete.

30. "Life, Liberty, and Justice for All Americans Act."

31. Ron Paul Institute, "Obama's Drone Strike: A Targeted Assassination," April 23, 2015, http://www.ronpaulinstitute.org/archives/featured-articles/2015/april/23/obamas-drone-strike-a-targeted-assassination/.

32. Jefferson Morley, "Another right-wing drone skeptic," *Salon*, June 1, 2012, http://www.salon.com/2012/06/01/another_right_wing_drone_skeptic/.

Conclusion

On May 1, 2016, international media reported that a British group known as the Islamic State Hacking Division released names and personal information on seventy individuals said to be members of US-based drone units active in the Middle East. The group called on adherents to go to the homes of these people and kill them. It was later reported that group founder Junaid Hussain had been killed in a drone strike in August 2015. The organization says they have a mole in the British Ministry of Defence and will in the future release names of drone operators in the Royal Air Force. They also temporarily gained control of the US Central Command's social media assets.[1]

These developments are not surprising and may only be the beginning as victims of drone warfare become increasingly able to retaliate. This particular threat may turn out to be empty bravado, but it is only a matter of time before the United States suffers its first attack on a "suburban barracks" in Nevada, Arizona, or elsewhere. Once the global-battlefield-as-everywhere is unleashed in the global South, it is doubtful that its spread can be limited. The global battlefield has arrived.

When this research was begun several years ago, the United States was at the beginning of a major expansion in the frequency and scope of drone warfare. Much of what is included here on this most fluid of topics was unknown to the authors then. And new information is becoming available all the time. As of this writing, four countries—the United States, United Kingdom, Israel, and Pakistan— have used weaponized drones in combat. There are three others that possess them, and at least ten others that are working on them. Remarkably, seventy-eight countries now have drone surveillance capacity. There is every reason to think that the ranks of weaponized drone powers will continue to swell.[2] While it was not widely reported, a weaponized Chinese CH-3 drone, carrying two air-to-surface missiles, crashed in northeast Nigeria in January 2015.[3]

All signs point to drone warfare as a transformative force in military affairs and in political life. The Western countries, led by the United States and United Kingdom, set the world on a path of permanent war, in part because military solutions are the only ones they seriously entertain. This is ironic given that relatively small terrorist attacks since the end of 2001 in the United States, United Kingdom, Spain, and France, created disruption far beyond their objective impact. It turns out that the liberal capitalist economy, the social system, the open culture, and constitutional, rights-oriented, liberal-democratic governance are all quite fragile.

The major challenge in the near future is not so much seeing what is right, but having the faith and confidence to transform the situation. Acceptance or resignation is the greatest ally of those who would employ destructive and self-defeating practices. The United States has faced down domestic adversity before—many times, in fact—and reformed itself. Despite confidence that this is an enlightened age, the argument in this concluding chapter is perhaps a shocking one— that US foreign and domestic policy is cruder and more ruthless now than it was in the Vietnam era. This means that the moral challenge Americans face today is even greater than that faced in the 1960s. The fierceness and resulting death toll of the Phoenix program in Vietnam is legendary, but parallels exist to today's global war on terrorism. Unlike Vietnam, there have so far been few vigorous protests, but that too could change. Clearly, the ultimate lesson of the Phoenix program and of the Vietnam War more generally, is that when American citizens understand the brutal acts of their government they will rise up and demand change. That is our potential for the future.

US PHOENIX PROGRAM IN VIETNAM:
THINGS CAN ALWAYS GET WORSE

Assassination is not new to the United States or other Western countries. The US government was heavily involved in plotting the assassinations of Congo's Patrice Lumumba, Vietnam's Ngo Diem, Cuba's Fidel Castro, Chile's General René Schneider, and, more recently, bin Laden and Qaddafi. Leaders like Salvador Allende (Chile) have been conveniently killed during US-backed *coups d'etat*. The highest body count in the last fifty years in an assassination operation was during the Phoenix program in Vietnam from 1967 to 1971. It was an early example of "manhunting,"[4] especially in the context of an inter-state war involving the United States, North Vietnam, and South Vietnam. Even in the context of a war in which three million Vietnamese were killed, much of the academic literature notes the brutality of the program. Gabriella Blue and Philip Heymann refer to it as one of "planned assassination,"[5] and Michael Gross refers to it as "widely condemned."[6] Dissident US intellectual Noam Chomsky writes of the Phoenix program frequently, citing figures of between forty thousand and forty-eight thousand killed, though he also notes that roughly an equivalent number was imprisoned for a time or switched allegiances to the South Vietnamese government side.

It is worth noting that atrocities in Vietnam were so widespread that one can write a critically oriented book on the war with almost no mention of Phoenix, as Nick Turse has recently done.[7] But contemporary killings, such as drone attacks in Afghanistan, Pakistan, Yemen, and elsewhere, *are actually worse* than the conduct of US and Vietnamese forces in the Phoenix program, from the perspective of lack of due process and the indiscriminate nature of the strikes.

Any discussion of the US war in Vietnam must address that conflict's highly contested nature. For American conservatives it was a noble effort and a winnable war that the United States chose not to win. For liberals and the left it was inherently immoral, based on an act of aggression, intervention in a civil war, and part of the US Cold War effort against the Soviet Union and China. The Vietnamese people mattered little. (The US government knew so little about the Soviet Union and China in the early 1960s that it didn't even understand the tensions and fissures between those soon-to-be former allies.) The West still does not understand that era from the Vietnamese perspective because a history based on Vietnamese experiences has not yet filtered into Western consciousness. Western literature either condemns the program for the body count or defends it as a good attempt to undermine the revolutionary movement that supported the military operations of the Viet Cong (as they were called in the United States).

Perhaps the most comprehensive source is *The Phoenix Program* by Douglas Valentine. He condemns the program based on interviews with former Phoenix operatives from the CIA and the US uniformed services. The United States worked with military forces of the pro-US Republic of Vietnam to apprehend or kill members of the civilian Viet Cong infrastructure (VCI), to deny supplies, intelligence, and recruits to the armed struggle. As Valentine says, and confirmed by more sympathetic observers, the program was plagued by US incompetence and lack of understanding of Vietnamese society, corruption of the South Vietnamese regime, inability to deal adequately with civilian detainees, personal vendettas, Vietnamese hedging and half-hearted efforts, and weak indigenous legal systems.[8]

The book that deserves greater attention, however, is *Ashes to Ashes: The Phoenix Program and the Vietnam War*, by Dale Andradé.[9] This work is fascinating although it considers the program a "well-intentioned but flawed effort." It does concede many critics' points regarding the role of the US

military, the corruption of the South Vietnam regime, and the edge in democratic legitimacy possessed by Ho Chi Minh's revolutionary movement. (Its
back-cover endorsement is by William Colby, 1973–1975 CIA director and a
senior manager of the Phoenix program in the late '60s.) The author takes
power politics for granted and doesn't mind agreeing with critics, to some
degree, regarding the nasty details of the war. This underappreciated source
provides us with a detailed view that concedes rather than denies problems. It
marshals a more spirited defense of the Phoenix program than can be presented by a contemporary defender of the George W. Bush-Obama drone
warfare doctrine. The implication is that in its current system of assassination, including the use of drone aircraft, the United States is conducting itself
in a worse fashion than it did in Vietnam. This is primarily because, at its
heart, Phoenix was not just an assassination program, but it also had significant law-enforcement and judicial elements missing from contemporary US
foreign policy. Many of the Vietnam-era problems Valentine highlights, and
Andradé admits, ring familiar for those who have followed the US efforts in
Afghanistan, Iraq, and other Middle Eastern countries since 9/11. If the United States could learn from the Phoenix experience and change at least for a
time, then the same thing can happen today.

Andradé writes that 1967 and 1968 were challenging years in Vietnam.
He notes that Ho Chi Minh would have won united elections in 1956, agreed
under the Geneva Accords, had they been allowed. He adds that the United
States and Government of (South) Viet Nam (GVN) militaries thought the
main challenge in the mid-1960s would be a conventional military one, even
though it took the form of a guerrilla war. The military was the dominant US
actor in Vietnam and was unwilling to change its tactics. One reason the
French failed in the 1946–54 period, Andradé confirms, was its opposition to
any kind of reform and its desire for a "return of the old inequitable ways of
running village affairs."[10]

Like other countries operating in the global South, the United States was
slow to understand that a guerrilla force or insurgency could only be effective if the *infrastructure* lying beneath it is effective—one of the insights
available at that time in Chinese leader Mao Zedong's *Little Red Book*. The
infrastructure was composed of noncombatant individuals who raised money
and supplied food and other material for the guerrilla force, and provided
intelligence on the movements of the enemy's conventional military forces.
Andradé says the relative success of the British counterinsurgency operation
in Malaysia was in part because the British treated the issue as a law-enforcement challenge rather than a military one. In the early 1950s the British gave
landless peasants land in "new villages," which were fenced. (Unsuccessful
efforts were made to replicate this in Vietnam in the early 1960s with the
Strategic Hamlets program.) The British then expanded the police force to
sixty thousand (from nine thousand) and ensured a police presence at all

times. This prevented the operation of the *Min Yuen* infrastructure, essential for the success of the armed insurgency in Malaysia.[11]

Andradé recognizes that before Diem was assassinated in 1963, he and his ruling clique were also part of the problem. While there were recommendations in the late 1950s to set up a strong rural police force along the lines of the Malay model, Diem refused because he believed that this force could rival his army and threaten his rule. Instead, Andradé tells us, Diem engaged in a counter-insurgency process running "the entire gamut of brutality: kidnappings, assassination, extortion, anything Diem felt was necessary to eliminate the communists in the villages. . . . Diem failed to realize that the use of such indiscriminate methods could only result in an increase in sympathy for the communist insurgency." The United States created Counter-Terrorism Teams, but Andradé notes that their effectiveness was limited because they were known to be CIA- (i.e., foreign-) controlled. Also, South Vietnamese government officials did not accept the need to undermine the VCI. The Vietnamese peasantry considered the CIA indistinguishable from the Diem regime, which itself was seen to have followed the path established by the French colonial power before it left Vietnam in 1954.[12]

By 1967, in the context of the deteriorating military situation, the US government came to the conclusion that pacification, as efforts to undermine the VCI were called, was as important as conventional military conflict between GVN/US and National Liberation Front (NLF)/North Vietnamese forces. A new joint civilian-military effort was headed by Robert "Blowtorch" Komer, to be called, euphemistically, Civil Operations and Revolutionary Development Support. It would make use of existing police and military assets, such as the Provincial Reconnaissance Units. American advisors worked alongside trained Vietnamese. In the Vietnamese language the program was called the *Phung Hoang*, named for a mythological bird; the closest term in English was the Phoenix, from ancient Middle Eastern mythology.

Phoenix teams sometimes conducted cordon-and-search operations where they would surround a village and search for evidence of VCI and supplies, literature, weapons, or tunnel networks. They would often receive information regarding individuals who joined or supported VCI, and they would embark on kill-or-capture raids. Andradé downplays the assassinations, though he does admit that there were considerable numbers killed. He focuses on the great numbers arrested for being VCI supporters, who were interrogated, and then tried and convicted or acquitted. He argues that "neutralization" was not at this time a synonym for "killed," but also referred to those captured and held for a time. It also included those who abandoned a civilian or military role in the insurgency and rallied to the government side. He cites official figures showing that in 1969, for example, 19,534 individuals were neutralized, either by being killed (6,187), captured (8,515), or coming over to the government side (4,832).[13] Andradé does not provide figures for the total killed, but forty thousand or more is certainly believable.

It is instructive that the accused Vietnamese in the late 1960s generally had more rights and protections than adversaries today in Guantanamo, Afghanistan, Pakistan, or elsewhere. The GVN ran *Chieu Hoi* (Open Arms), an amnesty program for those willing to quit the National Liberation Front or North Vietnamese military; 130,000 did so from 1963 to 1973, according to official figures.[14] Andradé spends a chapter on the courts and detention systems in Phoenix for those not willing to rally.[15] What becomes clear was that though efforts were made to establish a proper legal system at the policy level, it functioned imperfectly because of the shortage of educated lawyers and judges, and the resulting long delays and corruption. Contrast this with the contemporary global war on terrorism, where policy is nonexistent or repugnant.

Authorities were allowed to arrest suspects under the rubric of the Phoenix program based on earlier decrees declaring a state of emergency, state of war, and outlawing of certain organizations in South Vietnam. (It should be remembered that the GVN was itself illegitimate, a product of US eagerness to prevent the Vietnamese "domino" from falling to the "international communist conspiracy.") While warrants were required to arrest targeted, named individuals—and some Phoenix killings were the result of resistance to these arrests—it was also possible for warrants to be issued after the arrest.[16] Individuals then appeared before screening committees made up of Vietnamese, who were to act within days. They could either declare detainees innocent and release them, or declare them members of an "enemy military organization," to be sent to custody as POWs under the Geneva Conventions.

The screening committee could also declare them members of the VCI, which meant they would be directed to what the Vietnamese called the *an tri* system. Government had to prove that the detainees were members or supporters of the VCI based on a dossier that could include captured documents, eyewitness statements, intelligence reports, and confessions. A confession alone was not enough evidence to convict, and at least three eyewitness accounts were needed. A senior VCI cadre could be imprisoned for two years, while a lesser supporter could be sentenced for less than two years.[17]

It should be no surprise that there would be major problems with this system, some of which have been repeated more recently in the Middle East. In some cases corrupt officials would round up innocent people and force them to pay for their release[18]; some individuals would bear false witness to settle a score with a personal enemy. Further, there were torture and summary executions, which the US military actively opposed only under pressure from domestic anti-war groups.[19] There were very few lawyers in rural Vietnam, not even in the capital, Saigon (now Ho Chi Minh City), resulting in a lack of experience in conducting legal proceedings. Perhaps because of this, people languished in detention far too long. The detention centers became rich recruiting grounds for the VCI and the Viet Cong military wing that could easily convince the innocent that fundamental changes in Vietnamese society were necessary.

Government officials were aware of these problems. Deputy Undersecretary of the Army James V. Siena traveled to Vietnam in August 1969 to report on the Phoenix program. Andradé reports his reactions as follows:

> Siena gave the example of one highly regarded province chief who refused to back the Phoenix program and made no secret of his reasons for doing so. In his view the program, "exacts too high a price in social stability for the return it yields." He pointed out that most of the VCI neutralized by Phoenix were not ideologically committed to communism and they were not regarded as "bad men" by their fellow citizens. Delving into the sociological roots of the war in Vietnam, the province chief noted that becoming "a VC or an ARVN soldier depends on who was in control when you became old enough to bear arms."[20]

Andradé also notes that "uncertainty of the future" concerned Vietnamese on both sides. While US military and other personnel were expected to leave Vietnam eventually, the Vietnamese people realized that "[t]oday's VCI might become tomorrow's political leaders and there was a reluctance on the part of many provincial GNV officials to 'make life miserable now for someone who might be a legitimate political power in the future'."[21] Consequently, when the Vietnamese were in charge, there might have been shorter sentences, amnesties, and collusion in prison breaks based on officials' divided loyalties and the need to hedge bets. Douglas Valentine also relates a story from an interviewee about a tacit agreement among the Vietnamese that families were off limits—high-ranking officials on both sides would travel openly and not be traced through their families; nor would their families be attacked.[22] Many of these problems will also be familiar to those following internal dynamics of Afghanistan since 2001, and Iraq since 2003.

By 2012, the speeches of Obama officials, including former attorney general Eric Holder and John Brennan, indicated ways in which the current US assassination program has even fewer safeguards than Phoenix. As Glen Greenwald points out, in defending assassination, including of American citizens, Holder is on the record as saying that "due process and 'judicial process' are not one and the same, particularly when it comes to national security. The Constitution guarantees due process, not judicial process." This is an extreme view, every bit as extreme as some of the Bush administration positions. The idea that the test of due process is met by a process within the CIA, Joint Special Operations Command, or the West Wing of the White House, flies in the face of hundreds of years of the rule of law. It was revealed that, despite an "executive order banning assassinations, a federal law against murder, [and] protections in the Bill of Rights and various strictures of the international laws of war," Brennan led a unit in the White House in 2012 to recommend names that the president could then add to the kill list.[23] There is no legal basis for this, no role for an independent prosecutor or judiciary, and no appeal. The definitions of militant and terrorist and member of al-Qaeda are simply devised by the Executive Branch and subject to change and variation in interpretation. More recent reporting indicates that the Defense Department has been sidelined.[24] There is little emphasis on capturing rather than killing, little oversight, little cooperation with the locals, and no belief in rehabilitation.

Phoenix had certain features that compare favorably to US and Western policy in the global war on terrorism. Captured insurgents were treated as POWs, not as unlawful combatants. Detainees had a legal right to hearings. There were limits on sentences and recognition of the possibility of rehabilitation. In Vietnam there was a stronger element of a police or law-enforcement role, in contrast to the war on terrorism in which the solution is almost always a military one. There appears to have been greater US willingness to cooperate with the Vietnamese, even if Vietnam was considered a puppet of the United States. In Afghanistan or Pakistan, no amount of public complaining about drone attacks or night raids, makes any impact. Western countries are so powerful they don't even need the pretense of the host countries' consent to do as they wish. By 1975, the US military and diplomats left Vietnam, having lost. The most important lesson was that, as discussed earlier in this book, US voters sent a loud and clear message to Congress and the president that "presidential war" needed to end. The public demanded that the US government restrain successive officeholders from taking the same actions that caused so much grief for so many in the previous twenty-five years. Surely the citizens of the United States, and elsewhere, can have this kind of impact again.

GOING BACK TO THE DRAWING BOARD

Who really believes that the West can "win" this battle? How long will it take? What will the toll be in lost lives of combatants and civilians? Will society be recognizable by the time it happens? The West must go back to the drawing board to rethink this campaign known as the global war on terrorism. While there are truly odious people in the world, they have only become more numerous and powerful. Clearly the war on terrorism is not working, apart from the idea that some are gaining on a purely short-term basis. For economic and geopolitical reasons, the Western countries, led by the United States and the United Kingdom but with many other culpable allies, have sown chaos and carnage through the Middle East, with no regard for the medium- to long-term impact—or for the unintended but predictable consequences. It is instructive to look at recent history. Consider the last fifteen or thirty-five years, going back to the fateful decision of the Carter administration to impose on the Soviet Union its own Vietnam in Afghanistan.

World War II was a calamity of the twentieth century but one that ushered in a new world, a world better than the one that preceded it. This included the United Nations and its Charter, an elaborate system of international law, the Keynesian Welfare State, newly decolonized countries with their own nationalist and developmental agendas, and ironically, the stability created by the nuclear deterrence of the two adversarial superpowers.

There could be another disaster ahead, a bleak period for the human spirit and soul, and one that does not necessarily hold any glimmers of a better world. The Western intellectual tradition is largely optimistic. In dialectical thought it is posited that over time there is an upward trend in wealth and income, human freedom, enlightenment, and so on. But today perhaps is the moment of Giambatista Vico, the eighteenth-century Italian historian and philosopher, who understood that the human condition can go into long periods of degeneration, that progress can be lost, and that regeneration is far from automatic.[25]

The myriad of forces backing the transition to Drone Nation are formidable: think tanks, military contractors, media, government officials, permanent war advocates, the intelligence community, and corporate investors. In addition to all other challenges, domestic and international, taking control of assassination and drone warfare demands society's engagement and long-term commitment. It won't be easy but it will be necessary.

NOTES

1. Tom Wyke, "ISIS hacking division release names and personal details of dozens of American soldiers," *The Daily Mail*, May 1, 2016, http://www.dailymail.co.uk/news/article-3567944/ISIS-hacking-division-release-names-personal-details-dozens-American-soldiers-urging-lone-wolf-attacks.html#ixzz47SMfjv5E.

2. New America, "World of Drones: Military," n.d., http://securitydata.newamerica.net/world-drones.html. This site has an updated world map showing the drone status of countries throughout the world.

3. Adam Rawnsley, "It seems a Chinese Missile Drone just crashed in Nigeria," War is Boring, January 28, 2015, https://medium.com/war-is-boring/whose-drone-just-crashed-in-nigeria-c8c55bdf3476.

4. Grégoire Chamayou, *Theory of the Drone*, 32.

5. Gabriella Blum and Philip Heymann, "Law and Policy of Targeted Killing," *Harvard National Security Journal* 1(2010): 145–170.

6. Michael L. Gross, *Moral Dilemmas of Modern War: Torture, Assassination, and Blackmail in an Age of Asymmetric Conflict*, New York: Cambridge University, 2010.

7. Nick Turse, *Kill Anything That Moves: The Real American War in Vietnam* (New York: Metropolitan Books/Henry Holt and Company, 2013).

8. Douglas Valentine, *The Phoenix Program* (New York: William Morrow and Co., Inc., 1990), especially 151, 226–34.

9. Dale Andradé, *Ashes to Ashes: The Phoenix Program and the Vietnam War*, (Lexington, MA: Lexington Books, 1990).

10. Ibid., 6, 7, 13, 19.

11. Ibid., 23–26.

12. Ibid., 37, 38, 44.

13. Ibid., 129.

14. Ibid., 4.

15. Ibid., chapter 9.

16. Ibid., 214.

17. Ibid., 216–17.

18. Ibid., 67

19. Ibid., 211.

20. Ibid., 218.

21. Ibid.

22. Valentine, *Phoenix*, 233–34.

23. Glenn Greenwald, "How extremism is normalized," *Salon.com*, May 30, 2012.

24. Kimberley Dozier, "Who will drones target? Who in the US will decide?" Associated Press, *Salon.com* , May 21, 2012.

25. The scholarly literature by and about Vico is voluminous, but his classic work is entitled *The New Science*.

Bibliography

Abizaid, John, and R. Brooks. "Recommendations and Report of the Task Force on Drone Policy." Stimson Center, June 24, 2014. http://www.stimson.org/content/recommendations-and-report-stimson-task-force-us-drone-policy-0.

Ackerman, Evan. "Poll Shows Concern about Drones and Domestic Surveillance," IEEE Spectrum. June 25, 2012. http://spectrum.ieee.org/automaton/robotics/military-robots/poll-shows-concern-about-drones-and-domestic-surveillance.

Ackerman, Spencer. "US senators remove requirement for disclosure over drone strike victims." *The Guardian*, April 28, 2014. http://www.theguardian.com/world/2014/apr/28/drone-civilian-casualties-senate-bill-feinstein-clapper.

———. "West Point professor calls on US military to target legal critics of war on terror." *The Guardian*, August 29, 2015. http://www.theguardian.com/us-news/2015/aug/29/west-point-professor-target-legal-critics-war-on-terror?CMP=share_btn_tw.

Agence France-Presse. "US Air Force Lacks Volunteers to Operate Drones," August 21, 2013.

Alston, Philip. "Study on Targeted Killings: Report of the Special Rapporteur on extrajudicial, summary or arbitration executions." New York: United Nations General Assembly, Human Rights Council, May 28, 2010.

Alston, P., and E. MacDonald, eds. *Human Rights, Intervention and the Use of Force*. Oxford: Oxford University Press, 2008.

Altman, Andrew, and Christopher Heath Wellman. "From Humanitarian Intervention to Assassination: Human Rights and Political Violence." *Ethics* 118(2 [2008]): 228–57.

Anderson, Kenneth. "Targeted Killing in U.S. Counterterrorism Strategy and Law." *Legislating the War on Terror: An Agenda for Reform* edited by Benjamin Wittes. Washington, DC: Brookings Institution Press, 2009.

Andradé, Dale. *Ashes to Ashes: The Phoenix Program and the Vietnam War*. Lexington, MA: Lexington Books, 1990.

Arkin, Ronald. "Governing Lethal Behavior: Embedding Ethics in a Hybrid Deliberative/Reactive Robot Architecture." 7–8. http://www.cc.gatech.edu/ai/robot-lab/online-publications/formalizationv35.pdf.

Aron, Raymond. *The Imperial Republic*, Englewood Cliffs, NJ: Prentice Hall, 1974.

Asaro, Peter M. "The labor of surveillance and bureaucratized killing: New subjectivity of military drone operators." *Social Semiotics* 23(2): 196–224.

Astore William. "The Drone Medal." Huffington Post, July 13, 2012. http://www.huffingtonpost.com/william-astore/the-drone-medal_b_1671481.html.

Atherton, Kelsey D. "Air Force Will Let Enlisted Pilots Fly Global Hawks: An old lesson in manpower learned anew." *Popular Science,* December 21, 2015. http://www.popsci.com/air-force-will-let-enlisted-pilots-fly-global-hawks.

———. "Pentagon Agrees to Recognize Drone Pilots with a Decoration (Not quite a medal)." *Popular Science*, January 7, 2016. http://www.popsci.com/pentagon-agrees-to-recognize-drone-pilots-with-not-quite-medal.

Aussareses, Paul. *The Battle of the Casbah: Terrorism and Counter-Terrorism in Algeria, 1955–57.* New York: Enigma Books, 2002.

Axe, David. "How to Prevent Drone Pilot PTSD: Blame the 'Bot.'" *Wired,* June 7, 2012.

Baldor, Lolita. "Pentagon Creating New Medal For Drones, Cyberattacks." Spokesman, February 13, 2013, http://www.spokesman.com/stories/2013/feb/14/pentagon-creating-new-medal-for-cyber-drone/.

Barron, David. Memorandum for the Attorney General Re: Applicability of Federal Criminal Laws and the Constitution to Contemplated Lethal Operations Against Shaykh Anwar al-Aulaqi. Department of Justice, Office of Legal Counsel, July 16, 2010. http://cdn1.voxcdn.com/assets/4656273/dronememo.pdf.

Belfield, Richard. *The Assassination Business: A History of State-Sponsored Murder.* New York: Carroll and Graf Publishers, 2005.

Benen, Steve. "Rand Paul's drone 'evolution' now complete." The Maddow Blog, April 27, 2015. http://www.msnbc.com/rachel-maddow-show/rand-pauls-drone-evolution-now-complete.

Benson, Thor. "Five Ways We Must Restrict Drones at the US Border." *Wired,* May 20, 2015. http://www.wired.com/2015/05/drones-at-the-border/.

Bergen, Peter. "Drone Wars: The Constitutional and Counterterrorism Implications of Targeted Killing." New America, April 24, 2014. https://www.newamerica.org/international-security/testimony-drone-wars/.

Bergen, Peter, and J. Rowlands. "Civilian casualties plummet in drone strikes." CNN, July 14, 2012. http://www.cnn.com/2012/07/13/opinion/bergen-civilian-casualties/.

Bhatt, Chetan. "Human Rights and the Transformation of War." *Sociology* (2012) 46(5): 813–828.

Blanc, Sabine. "Drone Activism Takes to the Sky," OWNI.EU, March 13 2012.

Blodget, Henry. "U.S. Drone Pilot Explains What It's Like When You Realize You Just Killed a Kid." *Business Insiders,* May 13, 2013.

Blum, Gabriella, and Philip Heymann. "Law and Policy of Targeted Killing." *Harvard National Security Journal* 1(2010): 145–70.

Boseley, Sarah. "Drones should be included in arms reduction treaties, says medical charity." *The Guardian,* October 13, 2012. http://www.theguardian.com/world/2012/oct/13/drones-arms-reduction-treaties.

Boyle, Francis Anthony. *World Politics and International Law.* Durham, NC: Duke University Press, 1985.

Branfman, Fred. "Even the Warriors Say the Wars Make Us Less Safe." WorldBeyondWar.org. http://worldbeyondwar.org/lesssafe/.

Brennan, John. "The Ethics and Efficacy of the President's Counterterrorism Strategy." Woodrow Wilson Center for Scholars. Washington, DC, April 30, 2012.

Brenner, Aaron, R. Brenner, and C. Winslow, eds. *Rebel Rank and File: Labor Militancy and Revolt from Below in the Long 1970s.* London and New York: Verso, 2010.

Byers, Michael. *War Law: Understanding International Law and Armed Conflict.* New York: Grove Press, 2005.

Cameron, M.A., R. J. Lawson, and B. W. Tomlin, eds. *To Walk Without Fear: The Global Movement to Ban Landmines,* Toronto: Oxford University Press, 1998.

Canadian Press. "Omar Khadr timeline: A chronology of Omar Khadr's life and his long legal odyssey." *Toronto Star*, April 24, 2015. http://www.thestar.com/news/world/2015/04/24/omar-khadr-timeline.html.

Carroll, Chris. "Unmanned now undermanned: Air Force struggles to fill pilot slots for drones," Stripes, August 25, 2013. http://www.stripes.com/news/unmanned-now-undermanned-air-force-struggles-to-fill-pilot-slots-for-drones-1.236906.

CBS News. "Pentagon planning more drone usage over next several years." August 17, 2015, http://www.cbsnews.com/news/pentagon-planning-more-drone-usage-over-next-several-years/.

Chamayou, Grégoire. *A Theory of the Drone*. Translated by J. Lloyd. New York and London: The New Press, 2015.

Chandler, David. *From Kosovo to Kabul: Human Rights and International Intervention*. London and Sterling, VA: Pluto Press, 2002.

Chesney, Robert. "Shift to JSOC on Drone Strikes Does Not Mean CIA Has Been Sidelined." Lawfare, June 16, 2016. https://www.lawfareblog.com/shift-jsoc-drone-strikes-does-not-mean-cia-has-been-sidelined.

———. "Who May Be Killed? Anwar al-Awlaki as a Case Study in the International Legal Regulation of Lethal Force." *Yearbook of International Humanitarian Law* 13 (2010): 3–60.

Chu, Jennifer. "Driving drones can be a drag: Study shows distractions may alleviate boredom and improve drone operators' performance." November 14, 2012. http://phys.org/news/2012-11-distractions-alleviate-boredom-drone.html.

Cohn, Marjorie, and J. Mirer. "Killer Drone Attacks Illegal, Counter-Productive." Huffington Post, June 25, 2012. www.huffingtonpost.com.

Conniff, Richard."Drones are Ready for Takeoff : Will unmanned aerial vehicles—drones—soon take civilian passengers on pilotless flights?" *Smithsonian*, June 2011.

Conradis, Brandon. "Northrop Grumman's Drone Campaign." Center for Responsive Politics, November 8, 2013. http://www.opensecrets.org/news/2013/11/northrop-grummans-lobbying-campaign/.

Cox, Robert, and H. Jacobson. *The Anatomy of Influence: Decision Making in International Organization* New Haven, CT: Yale University Press, 1974.

CQ Almanac. "Defense 1982: Overview." https://library.cqpress.com/cqalmanac/document.php?id=cqal82-1163642.

Currier, Cora. "Who Are We at War With? That's Classified." *ProPublica*, July 26, 2013. http://www.propublica.org/article/who-are-we-at-war-with-thats-classified.

Dao, James. "Drone Pilots Are Found to Get Stress Disorders Much as Those in Combat Do." *New York Times*, February 22, 2013.

Dear, John, S. J. "A peace movement victory in court." *National Catholic Reporter*, September 21, 2010. http://www.fatherjohndear.org/articles/a-peace-movement-victory-in-court.html.

Dellums, Ronald V., with R. H. Miller and H. L. Halterman. *Defense Sense: The Search for a Rational Military Policy*. Cambridge, MA: Ballinger Publishing Company, 1983.

Development, Concepts and Doctrine Centre. *Global Strategic Trends-Out to 2045*. London, UK: Ministry of Defence, 2014. https://www.gov.uk/government/uploads/system/uploads/attachment_data/file/348164/20140821_DCDC_GST_5_Web_Secured.pdf.

Devereaux, Ryan. "Obama Administration Finally Releases Its Dubious Drone Death Toll." *The Intercept*, July 1, 2016. https://theintercept.com/2016/07/01/obama-administration-finally-releases-its-dubious-drone-death-toll/.

Dillingham, Gerald L."Unmanned Aircraft Systems; Use in the national airspace system and the role of the Department of Homeland Security." United States Government Accountability Office, July 19, 2012.

Domhoff, G. William. *Who Rules America? The Triumph of the Corporate Rich*. 7th ed. New York: McGraw Hill Education, 2014.

Dozier, Kimberley. "Who will drones target? Who in the US will decide?." Associated Press, *Salon.com*, May 21, 2012.

Dunnigan, James. "Pilots Despise Flying UAVs." Strategy Page, August 30, 2012. https://www.strategypage.com/dls/articles/Pilots-Despise-Flying-UAVs-8-30-2012.asp.

European Section, Global Anti-Drone Network. "'Ban Weaponized Drones': Anti-Drone Movement Spreads in Europe." Truthout, December 19, 2013. http://www.truth-out.org/speakout/item/20740-ban-weaponized-drones-anti-drone-movement-spreads-in-europe.

Fang, Lee. "Who's Paying the Pro-War Pundits?" *The Nation*, September 16, 2014. https://www.thenation.com/article/whos-paying-pro-war-pundits/.

Ferenstein, Gregory. "Weaponized Drones for Law Enforcement Now Legal in North Dakota." *Forbes*, August 25, 2015. http://www.forbes.com/sites/gregoryferenstein/2015/08/26/weaponized-drones-now-legal-inside-the-u-s-lawmaker-says-crimefighting-will-become-a-video-game/#77ee93e37a57.

Fielding-Smith, Abigail, Crofton Black, Alice Ross, and James Ball. "Revealed: Private firms at heart of US drone warfare." *The Guardian*, July 30, 2015. http://www.theguardian.com/us-news/2015/jul/30/revealed-private-firms-at-heart-of-us-drone-warfare.

Forrester, Anna. "Northrop Grumman to Deliver 5 Global Hawks to NATO." *ExecutiveBiz*, January 27, 2016. http://blog.executivebiz.com/2016/01/defense-news-nato-air-base-in-italy-to-take-in-5-northrop-global-hawks-by-years-end/.

Franceschi-Bicchierai, Lorenzo. "Drone Hijacking? That's Just the Start of GPS Troubles." *Wired*, July 6, 2012.

Friedersdorf, Conor. "Flawed Analysis of Drone Strike Data Is Misleading Americans." *The Atlantic*, July 18, 2012, http://www.theatlantic.com/politics/archive/2012/07/flawed-analysis-of-drone-strike-data-is-misleading-americans/259836/.

Fuller, Christopher J. "The Eagle Comes Home to Roost: The Historical Origins of the CIA's Lethal Drone Program." *Intelligence and National Security*, 2015. doi: 10.1080/02684527.2014.895569.

Fung, Brian. "Why drone makers have declared war on the word 'drone.'" *Washington Post*, August 16, 2013. http://www.washingtonpost.com/blogs/the-switch/wp/2013/08/16/why-drone-makers-have-declared-war-on-the-word-drone/.

Gent, Edd. "The Future of Drones: Uncertain, Promising and Pretty Awesome." Livescience.com, November 5, 2015. http://www.livescience.com/52701-future-of-drones-uncertain-but-promising.html.

Gilsinan, Kathy. "The Drone War Crosses Another Line," *The Atlantic*, May 23, 2016. http://www.theatlantic.com/international/archive/2016/05/drone-mullah-akhtar-taliban/483863/.

Glad, Betty. *An Outsider in the White House: Jimmy Carter, His Advisors and the Making of American Foreign Policy*. Ithaca, NY: Cornell University Press, 2009.

Gould, Elizabeth, and Paul Fitzgerald. *Crossing Zero: The AFPAK War at the Turning Point of American Empire*. San Francisco: City Light Books, 2011.

Grant, George. *Lament for a Nation: The Defeat of Canadian Nationalism*. 1965 essay. Montreal-Kingston: McGill-Queen's UP, 2005.

Green, Michael, and Gladys Green. *Remotely Piloted Aircraft: The Predators*. Mankato, MN: Capstone Press, 2004.

Greenberg, Andy. "Hacker Says He Can Hijack a $35K Police Drone a Mile Away." *Wired*, March 3, 2016. http://www.wired.com/2016/03/hacker-says-can-hijack-35k-police-drone-mile-away/.

Greenwald, Glenn. "The Brookings Institution demands servile journalism." *The Guardian*, October 15, 2012. http://www.theguardian.com/commentisfree/2012/oct/15/drones-brookings-media.

———. "'Militants': media propaganda." *Salon*, May 29, 2012. http://www.salon.com/2012/05/29/militants_media_propaganda/.

———. "NYT Claims U.S. Abides by Cluster Bomb Treaty: The Exact Opposite of Reality." *The Intercept*, September 3, 2015. https://theintercept.com/2015/09/03/nyt-claims-u-s-abides-cluster-bomb-ban-exact-opposite-reality/.

Gregory, Derek. "From a View to a Kill: Drones and Late Modern War." *Theory, Culture and Society* 28(7–8[2011]): 188–215.

Gross, Michael. "Assassination and Targeted Killing: Law Enforcement, Execution or Self-Defence?" *Journal of Applied Philosophy* 23(3 [2006]): 323–35.

———. *Moral Dilemmas of Modern War: Torture, Assassination, and Blackmail in an Age of Asymmetric Conflict*. New York: Cambridge University, 2010.

Grover, William. "Deep Presidency: Toward a Structural Theory of an Unsustainable Office in a Catastrophic World—Obama and Beyond." *New Political Science* 35(3 [2013]), 432–48. doi:10.1080/07393148.2013.813697.

Groves, Steven. "Drone Strikes: The Legality of U.S. Targeting Terrorists Abroad." The Heritage Foundation, April 10, 2013. http://www.heritage.org/research/reports/2013/04/drone-strikes-the-legality-of-us-targeting-terrorists-abroad.

Grut, Chantal, and Naureen Shah. *Counting Drone Strike Deaths*. New York: Human Rights Clinic, Columbia University, 2012.

Halliday, Fred. *The Making of the Second Cold War*. New York: Verso, 1987.

Harress, Christopher. "12 Companies That Will Conquer the Drone Market In 2014 and 2015." *International Business News*, January 10, 2014. http://www.ibtimes.com/12-companies-will-conquer-drone-market-2014-2015-1534360.

Hartung, William D. *Prophets of War: Lockheed Martin and the Making of the Military-Industrial Complex*. New York: Nation Books, 2012.

Hayden, Michael V. "To Keep America Safe, Embrace Drone Warfare." *New York Times*, February 19, 2016. http://www.nytimes.com/2016/02/21/opinion/sunday/drone-warfare-precise-effective-imperfect.html?_r=1.

Hoagland, Bradley C. *Manning the Next Unmanned Air Force: Selecting the Pilots of the Future*. Washington, DC: Brookings Institution, 2013.

Holmes, Robert L. *On War and Morality*. Princeton, NJ: Princeton University Press, 1989.

Holmqvist, Caroline. "Undoing War: War, Ontologies and the Materiality of Drone Warfare." *Millennium: Journal of International Studies* 41(3): 535–52.

Hughes, Stuart. "Campaigners call for international ban on 'killer robots.'" BBC, April 23, 2013. http://www.bbc.com/news/uk-22250664.

Humphreys, Todd. "Statement on the Vulnerability of Civil Unmanned Aerial Vehicles and Other Systems to Civil GPS Spoofing." Submitted to the Subcommittee on Oversight, Investigations, and Management of the House Committee on Homeland Security, July 18, 2012.

Jaffe, Greg. "How Obama went from reluctant warrior to drone champion." *Washington Post*, July 1, 2016. https://www.washingtonpost.com/politics/how-obama-went-from-reluctant-warrior-to-drone-champion/2016/07/01/a41dbd3a-3d53-11e6-a66f-aa6c1883b6b1_story.html.

Jansen, Bart. "FAA completes landmark rules for commercial drones." *USA Today*, June 21, 2016. http://www.usatoday.com/story/news/2016/06/21/faa-commercial-drone-rules/85641170/.

Johnson, Chalmers. *Blowback: The Costs and Consequences of American Empire*. 2nd edition. New York: Holt Paperbacks, 2004.

———. *Dismantling the Empire: America's Last Best Hope*. New York: Henry Holt and Company/ Metropolitan Books, 2010.

Johnson, James Turner. *Can Modern War Be Just?* New Haven and London: Yale University Press, 1984.

Jones, Seth. "Take the War to Pakistan." *New York Times*, December 3, 2009. http://www.nytimes.com/2009/12/04/opinion/04jones.html?_r=0.

Jordan, Bryant. "DoD Stands Behind Controversial Drone, Cyber Medal." February 20, 2013. http://www.military.com/daily-news/2013/02/20/dod-stands-behind-controversial-drone-cyber-medal.html.

Kaldor, Mary. *New and Old Wars: Organized Violence in a Global Era*. Stanford, CA: Stanford University Press, 1999.

Kendall, J. Nicholas. "Israeli Counter-Terrorism: 'Targeted Killings' Under International Law," *North Carolina Law Review* 80 (2002): 1069–88.

Kilkenny, Allison. "The brave armchair generals calling for Julian Assange's criminalization." Wearecitizenradio.com, 2010.

Kinsella, Helen M. *The Image before the Weapon: A Critical History of the Distinction between Combatant and Civilian*. Ithaca and London: Cornell University Press, 2011.

Klaidman, Daniel. "Drones: The Silent Killers." *Newsweek*, May 28, 2012. http://www.newsweek.com/drones-silent-killers-64909.

Koebler, Jason. "Teen Fights to Defend His Legal Right to Strap Guns to Drones." *Motherboard*, June 7, 2016. http://motherboard.vice.com/read/teen-fights-for-the-right-to-strap-guns-to-drones.

Kreps, Sarah. *Drones: What Everyone Needs to Know*. New York: Oxford University Press, 2016.

———. "Flying under the radar: A study of public attitudes towards unmanned aerial vehicles." *Research and Politics* April-June 2014: 1–7.

Kristof, Nicholas D. "Our Lefty Military." *New York Times*, June 15, 2011. http://www.nytimes.com/2011/06/16/opinion/16kristof.html?_r=0.

Ledbetter, James. *Unwarranted Influence: Dwight D. Eisenhower and the Rise of the Military-Industrial Complex.* New Haven and London: Yale University Press, 2011.

Lewis, Michael W., and Vincent J. Vitkowsk. "The Use of Drones and Targeted Killing in Counterterrorism." www.fed-soc.org.

Lofgren, Mike. *The Deep State: The Fall of the Constitution and the Rise of a Shadow Government.* New York: Viking, 2016.

Logan, Lara. "America's New Air Force." *60 Minutes.* May 10, 2009.

Lomberg, Jason. "Do drone pilots deserve higher medal than combat vets?" February 20, 2013. https://www.ecnmag.com/article/2013/02/do-drone-pilots-deserve-higher-medal-combat-vets.

MacLeod, I. J. and A. P. V. Rogers, "The Use of White Phosphorus and the Law of War." *Yearbook of International Humanitarian Law* X (75–97 [2007]).

Martin, Geoff and Erin Steuter. *Pop Culture Goes to War: Enlisting and Resisting Militarism in the War on Terror.* Lanham, MD, USA: Lexington Books, 2010.

Martinez, Michael, John Newsome, and Rene Marsh. "Handgun-firing drone appears legal in video, but police, FAA probe." CNN, July 21, 2015. http://www.cnn.com/2015/07/21/us/gun-drone-connecticut/.

Mattise, Nathan. "Grandma repeatedly protested drones at base, now faces a year in jail." *Arstechnica,* July 13, 2014. http://arstechnica.com/tech-policy/2014/07/grandma-repeatedly-protested-drones-at-base-now-faces-a-year-in-prison/.

McCaney, Kevin. "A drone by any other name is . . . an RPA?" Defense Systems, May 23, 2014. http://defensesystems.com/articles/2014/05/23/dempsey-rpa-drones-uas.aspx.

McCann, James G. "Go to Global Think Tank Index Report, Think Tanks and Civil Societies Program (TTCSP)." University of Pennsylvania, 2015.

McCrisken, Trevor. "Obama's Drone War." *Survival: Global Politics and Strategy.* 55(2 [2013]): 97–122.

———. "Ten years on: Obama's war on terrorism in rhetoric and practice." *International Affairs* 87(4 [2011]): 781–801.

McKelvey, Tara. "Media Coverage of the Drone Program." Joan Shorenstein Center on the Press, Politics and Public Policy, Harvard University. Discussion Paper D-77, February 2013.

Medina, Daniel A. "Drone markets open in Russia, China and rogue states as America's wars wane." *The Guardian,* June 22, 2016. http://www.theguardian.com/business/2014/jun/22/drones-market-us-military-china-russia-rogue-state.

Medvetz, Thomas. *Think Tanks in America.* Chicago: University of Chicago Press, 2012.

Melzer, Nils. *Targeted Killing in International Law.* Oxford: Oxford University Press, 2008.

Menthe, Lance, Myron Hura, and Carl Rhodes. "The Effectiveness of Remotely Piloted Aircraft in a Permissive Hunter-Killer Scenario." Washington, DC: Rand Corporation, 2014. http://www.rand.org/content/dam/rand/pubs/research_reports/RR200/RR276/RAND_RR276.pdf.

Miller, Greg. U.S. launches secret drone campaign to hunt Islamic State leaders in Syria." *Washington Post,* September 1, 2015. https://www.washingtonpost.com/world/national-security/us-launches-secret-drone-campaign-to-hunt-islamic-state-leaders-in-syria/2015/09/01/723b3e04–5033–11e5–933e-7d06c647a395_story.html.

———. "Why CIA drone strikes have plummeted," *Washington Post,* June 16, 2016. https://www.washingtonpost.com/world/national-security/cia-drone-strikes-plummet-as-white-house-shifts-authority-to-pentagon/2016/06/16/e0b28e90–335f-11e6–8ff7–7b6c1998 b7a0_story.html?hpid=hp_hp-more-top-stories_drones-1045am%3Ahomepage%2Fstory.

Milstein, Michael. "*Pilot Not Included: Military aviation prepares for the inevitable." *Air and Space Magazine,* July 2011.

Mitchell, Greg. *So Wrong for So Long: How the Press, the Pundits—and the President—Failed on Iraq.* New York and London: Union Square Press, 2008.

Morgan, David, and Deepa Seetharaman. "Industry lobbyists take aim at proposed FAA drone rules." Reuters, February 23, 2016. http://www.reuters.com/article/us-usa-drones-lobbying-idUSKBN0LS04R20150224.

Morley, Jefferson. "Another right-wing drone skeptic." *Salon*, June 1, 2012. http://www.salon.com/2012/06/01/another_right_wing_drone_skeptic/.

Mueller, Karl, J. Castillo, F. Morgan, N. Pegahi, and B. Rosen. *First Strike: Preemptive and Preventative Attack in US National Strategic Policy*. Santa Monica, CA: RAND Corporation, 2006. http://www.rand.org/content/dam/rand/pubs/monographs/2006/RAND_MG403.pdf.

New America. "World of Drones: Military," n.d. http://securitydata.newamerica.net/worlddrones.html.

Niva, Steve. "Disappearing violence: JSOC and the Pentagon's new cartography of networked warfare," *Security Dialogue*. 44(3 [2013]): 185–212.

O'Connell, Mary Ellen. "Unlawful Killing with Combat Drones: A Case Study of Pakistan, 2004–2009." Notre Dame Law School Legal Studies Research paper Series 9(43 [2004]): 179–98.

Old Soldier Colonel Blog. "Drones—UAVs—RPVs: The Argument for Why They Are the Future of Military Aviation and Who Should be Flying Them!" August 5, 2012, http://oldsoldier-colonel.blogspot.ca/2012/08/drones-uavs-rpvs-argument-for-why-they.html.

Oreskes, Naomi and E. Conway. "Global Warming Deniers and Their Proven Strategy of Doubt." Environment 360, June 10, 2010. http://e360.yale.edu/feature/global_warming_deniers_and_their_proven_strategy_of_doubt/2285/.

Packer, Jeremy, and Joshua Reeves. "Romancing the Drone: Military Desire and Anthropophobia from SAGE to Swarm." *Canadian Journal of Communication* 38 (2013): 309–31.

Page, Lewis. "RAF graduates first class of new groundbased 'pilots.'" *The Register*, April 4, 2013.http://www.theregister.co.uk/2013/04/04/raf_drone_rpas_pilots_graduate/

Palmer, Brian. "Is It Hard to Kill a Drone? *Slate*, June 6, 2012.

Parenti, Michael. *The Face of Imperialism*. Boulder and London: Paradigm Publishers, 2011.

Paulsen, Michael Stokes. "Drone On: The Commander in Chief Power to Target and Kill Americans." *Harvard Journal of Law and Public Policy*. 38(1 [2014]): 43–61.

Pegues, Jeff. "Homeland Security warns drones could be used in attacks." CBS News, July 31, 2015. http://www.cbsnews.com/news/homeland-security-warns-drones-could-be-used-in-attacks/.

Porter, Gareth. "US: *Washington Post* Drone Story Ignored Pak Military Opposition to Strikes." *Global Information Network*, October 25, 2013.

Porter, Lindsay, *Assassination: A History of Political Murder*. London: Thames & Hudson Publishers, 2010.

Powell, Chris. "We Are Not Drones: Pilots, Sensor Operators Put Human Element in RPA Operations." *Airman*, October 21, 2013.

Primoratz, Igor, ed. *Civilian Immunity in War*. Oxford: Oxford University Press, 2007.

Professional Golf Association. "Military golf courses come under fire," December 22, 2012. http://www.pga.com/golf-courses/golf-buzz/military-golf-courses-come-under-fire.

Qureshi, Asim. "The 'Obama doctrine': Kill, don't detain." *The Guardian*, April 11, 2010.

Rawnsley, Adam. "It seems a Chinese Missile Drone just crashed in Nigeria: Is Beijing selling killer robots in Africa?" War is Boring, January 28, 2015. https://medium.com/war-is-boring/whose-drone-just-crashed-in-nigeria-c8c55bdf3476.

Reuters. "U.S. Government, Police Working on Counter-Drone Measures." Newsweek.com, August 20, 2015. http://www.newsweek.com/us-government-police-working-counter-drone-measures-364453.

Riopelle, Cameron, and Parthiban Muniandy. "Drones, maps and crescents: CBS News' visual construction of the Middle East." *Media, War and Conflict* 6(2): 153–172.

Rogan, Tom. "In Defense of Drones." *National Review*, October 21, 2013. http://www.nationalreview.com/article/361720/defense-drones-tom-rogan.

Ron Paul Institute. "Obama's Drone Strike: A Targeted Assassination." April 23, 2015. http://www.ronpaulinstitute.org/archives/featured-articles/2015/april/23/obamas-drone-strike-a-targeted-assassination/.

Ross, Alice. "Former US drone technicians speak out against programme in Brussels." *The Guardian,* July 1, 2016. https://www.theguardian.com/world/2016/jul/01/us-drone-whistleblowers-brussels-european-parliament.

Ross, Alice, and Owen Bowcott. "UK drone strikes 'could leave all those involved facing murder charges.'" *The Guardian*, May 10, 2016. http://www.theguardian.com/politics/2016/may/10/uk-drone-strikes-murder-charges-clarify-legal-basis-targeted-kill-policy-isis.

Royakkers, Lambér, and Rinie van Est. "The cubicle warrior: The marionette of digitalized warfare." *Ethics and Information Technology* 12 (2010): 289–96.

Rozenweig, Paul, S. Bucci, C. Stimson, and J. Carafano. "Drones in U.S. Airspace: Principles for Governance." The Heritage Foundation, September 20, 2012. http://www.heritage.org/research/reports/2012/09/drones-in-us-airspace-principles-for-governance.

Saletan, William. "Don't Blame Drones." *Slate*, April 24, 2015. http://www.slate.com/articles/news_and_politics/foreigners/2015/04/u_s_drone_strikes_civilian_casualties_would_be_much_higher_without_them.html.

Scahill, Jeremy. "The Assassination Complex." *The Intercept*, October 15, 2015. https://theintercept.com/drone-papers/.

———. "Kucinich: White House assassination policy is extrajudicial." *The Nation*, April 15, 2010.

———. "The Secret US War in Pakistan," *The Nation*, November 23, 2009.

Schofield, Rob. "Legislative committee on drones: Yet another ALEC-inspired front for industry?" The Pulse (NC Policy Watch), January 21, 2014. http://pulse.ncpolicywatch.org/2014/01/21/legislative-committee-on-drones-yet-another-alec-inspired-front-for-industry/.

Schogol, Jeff. "More unmanned aircraft pilots being promoted." Military Times, November 6, 2013. http://www.militarytimes.com/home/.

Shalal, Andrea. "Northrop wins U.S. Global Hawk drone contract worth up to $3.2 billion." Reuters, September 30, 2015. http://www.reuters.com/article/us-northrop-grumman-globalhawk-idUSKCN0RU2UT20150930.

———. "U.S. needs longer-range, stealthy drones: think tank." Reuters, December 9, 2014. http://www.reuters.com/article/2014/12/10/us-usa-military-technology-idUSKBN0JO08020141210.

Sharrer, Erica, and Greg Blackburn. "Images of Injury: Graphic News Visuals' Effects on Attitudes Toward the Use of Unmanned Drones." *Mass Communication and Society*, May 2015.

Shaw, Ian, and Majed Akhter. "The Dronification of State Violence." *Critical Asian Studies* 46(2 [2014]): 211–34. doi: 10.1080/14672715.2014.898452.

Shaw, Martin. *The New Western Way of War: Risk-Transfer War and Its Crisis in Iraq.* Cambridge, UK and Malden, MA: Polity Press, 2005.

Sirota, David. "It's Just Shocking What the Drone War Cheerleaders Are Willing to Say Out Loud." Alternet, February 4, 2013. http://www.alternet.org/world/its-just-shocking-what-drone-war-cheerleaders-are-willing-say-out-loud.

Smith, Josh. "Drones emerge from shadows to become key cog in U.S. war machine." Reuters, June 6, 2016. http://www.reuters.com/article/us-afghanistan-drones-insight-idUSKCN0YT0U0.

Somerstein, Rachel. "We can't remember what we haven't seen: Media, war and the future of collective memory." *Afterimage* 40(4 [Jan/Feb 2013]): 10–14.

Statman, Daniel. "Targeted Killing." *Theoretical Inquiries in Law* 5(1 [2004]): 179–98.

Steiner, H., P. Alston, and R. Goodman. *International Human Rights in Context: Law, Politics, Morals*, 3rd ed. Oxford: Oxford University Press, 2007.

Stepanovich, Amie, Electronic Privacy Information Center. "Testimony and Statement for the Record," submitted to the Subcommittee on Oversight, Investigations, and Management of the House Committee on Homeland Security, July 19, 2012.

Stone, Andrea. "Drone Privacy Bill Would Put in Safeguards on Surveillance." Huffington Post, August 2, 2012.

Supreme Court of the United States of America. Decision in *Hamdi v. Rumsfeld*, June 28, 2004, No. 03–6696. https://supreme.justia.com/cases/federal/us/542/507/#annotation.

Swanson, David. "A New Model Drone Resolution." *Counterpunch*, January 25, 2013. http://www.counterpunch.org/2013/01/25/a-new-model-drone-resolution/.

Swift, Christopher. "The Drone Blowback Fallacy." *Foreign Affairs*, July 1, 2012. https://www.foreignaffairs.com/articles/middle-east/2012-07-01/drone-blowback-fallacy.

Tenold, Vegas. "Badass Attorney Shoots Down the Case for Drones." *Rolling Stone*, February 24, 2016. http://www.rollingstone.com/politics/news/badass-attorney-shoots-down-the-case-for-drones-20160224.

———. "The Untold Casualties of the Drone War." *Rolling Stone*, February 18, 2016. http://www.rollingstone.com/politics/news/the-untold-casualties-of-the-drone-war-20160218.

Thompson, Mark. "Drone Pilots: No Worse Off Than Those Who Actually Fly." *Time*, April 2, 2013.

Thompson II, William M. "Drones in Domestic Surveillance Operations: Fourth Amendment Implications and Legislative Responses." *Congressional Research Service*, April 3, 2013. http://www.fas.org/sgp/crs/natsec/R42701.pdf.

Tirman, John. *The Deaths of Others: The Fate of Civilians in America's Wars*. Oxford and New York: Oxford University Press, 2011.

Turse, Nick. "A Drone-Eat-Drone World." *Z Magazine* XXV (7/8): 55–58.

———. *Kill Anything That Moves: The Real American War in Vietnam*. New York: Metropolitan Books/Henry Holt and Company, 2013.

US Department of State. "U.S. Export Policy for Military Unmanned Aerial Systems," February 17, 2015. http://www.state.gov/r/pa/prs/ps/2015/02/237541.htm.

US Department of State. *Foreign Relations of the United States, 1952–1954*. Vol. XIII: *Indochina*. Washington, DC: US Department of State, 1982.

US Senate. *United States Senate, Select Committee to Study Governmental Operations with Respect to Intelligence Activities. Alleged Assassination Plots Involving Foreign Leaders: An Interim Report*. New York: W. W. Norton, 1976.

Valentine, Douglas. *The Phoenix Program*. New York: William Morrow and Co., Inc., 1990.

Van Buren, Peter. "This Land Isn't Your Land, This Land Is Their Land." May 1, 2014, http://zcomm.org/znetarticle/this-land-isnt-your-land-this-land-is-their-land/.

Vico, Giambatista. *The New Science of Giambattista Vico*. Translated by T. G. Bergin and M. H. Fisch. Ithaca, NY: Cornell University Press, 1968.

Watson, Paul Joseph. "Surveillance drones blasted out of the sky in protest against 4th amendment intrusion." Infowars.com, May 29, 2012. http://www.infowars.com/drones-shot-down-over-texas/.

Wheeler, Marcy. "Key Area of Dispute on Drone Numbers: Number of Strikes." Empty-Wheel.net, July 13, 2016. http://www.commondreams.org/views/2016/07/13/key-area-dispute-drone-numbers-number-strikes.

White House. NSDD 138, April 4, 1984, 4. http://www.reagan.utexas.edu/archives/reference/Scanned%20NSDDS/NSDD138.pdf.

Whitlock, Craig. "Crashes mount as military flies more drones in U.S.," Pt. 2. Washington Post, June 22, 2014. http://www.washingtonpost.com/sf/investigative/2014/06/22/crashes-mount-as-military-flies-more-drones-in-u-s/.

Wight, Martin. "Why is there no International Theory?" *Diplomatic Investigations: Essays in the Theory of International Politics* edited by H. Butterfield and M. Wight, 17–34. London: George Allen and Unwin Ltd., 1966.

Williams, J., S. Goose and M. Wareham, eds. *Banning Landmines: Disarmament, Citizen Diplomacy and Human Security*. Lanham, MD: Rowman and Littlefield Publishers, 2008.

Wills, Garry. *Bomb Power: The Modern Presidency and the National Security State*. New York: The Penguin Press, 2010.

Wittes, Benjamin. "Very Strange Column by the *New York Times* Public Editor." Lawfare, October 15, 2012. http://www.lawfareblog.com/very-strange-column-new-york-times-public-editor.

———. "Why I Won't Engage Glenn Greenwald," *Lawfare*, January 16, 2011. http://www.lawfareblog.com/why-i-wont-engage-glenn-greenwald.

Woods, Chris. *Sudden Justice: America's Secret Drone Wars*. Oxford and New York: Oxford University Press, 2015.

Wyke, Tom. "ISIS hacking division release names and personal details of dozens of American soldiers urging lone wolf attacks," *The Daily Mail*, May 1, 2016. http://www.dailymail.co.uk/news/article-3567944/ISIS-hacking-division-release-names-personal-details-dozens-American-soldiers-urging-lone-wolf-attacks.html#ixzz47SMfjv5E.

Yenne, Bill. *Birds of Prey: Predators, Reapers and America's Newest UABs in Combat.* North Branch, MN: Specialty Press, 2010.

Yost, Peter. "Drone Strikes will continue despite EU Ban." *Russia Today*, February 28, 2014. http://www.rt.com/op-edge/eu-ban-on-drone-strikes-158/.

———. "Rep. Massie, Rep. Radel and Rep. Amash Introduce the Life, Liberty, and Justice for All Americans Act." *Thomas Massie United States Congress*, March 19. 2013. http://www.thomasmassie.com/2013/03/19/rep-massie-rep-radel-rep-amash-introduce-life-liberty-justice-americans-act/#.VdxscnmFMdV.

———."Rise of the Drones." *Nova*, January 23, 2013.

Zoroya, Gregg. "Pentagon report justifies deployment of military spy drones over the U.S." *USA Today*, March 9, 2016. http://www.usatoday.com/story/news/nation/2016/03/09/pentagon-admits-has-deployed-military-spy-drones-over-us/81474702/.

Index

About the Authors

Geoff Martin has been teaching political science for twenty-five years and conducts research on international relations and US foreign policy. A regular contributor on politics to local media, his published research articles have appeared in several books and noted academic journals such as the *International Political Science Review*.

Erin Steuter is professor of sociology at Mount Allison University with a focus on critical media studies and ideological representations in news and popular culture. Recipient of multiple awards for her teaching and research, her published works have appeared in *Reconstruction: Studies in Contemporary Culture, Journal of War and Culture Studies, Global Media Journal, Political Communication and Persuasion, Canadian Journal of Communication, Journal of American and Comparative Cultures*.

Lightning Source UK Ltd.
Milton Keynes UK
UKHW040709130219
337169UK00001B/41/P